EMMA JANE HARRISON

How We Manifest

Time for a change

First edition

ISBN: 978-1-4461-8433-2

This book was professionally typeset on Reedsy.
Find out more at reedsy.com

Contents

Introduction

Introduction

This book is aimed as a guidance and a helping hand. Changing mindsets from poverty to wealth and making it stick. We can become wealthy it's a matter of making it stick. All the money in the world could be shared equally but it will end up in the same places.

In order for it to stick, we must change our mindsets. We must be willing to change them in order for our circumstances to change and our life to improve. I have learned much from "The Secret" and Bob Proctor Including Spear business solutions. I have studied myself and looked closely at the behaviours of others. As I have grown and connected to my higher self. I have learned more about life's vibrations and how we are all connected in the realm of thought.

My aim in life and this book is to help as many people as possible. I know many of you have watched "The Secret", "Dare to Dream" and many others about The Law of Attraction and changing mindsets. Never changing our mindsets as we don't know how. There are numerous books and podcasts out there on this subject.

I thought I would try to make it even simpler. How many times have you looked in the mirror and said that "I am going to change and improve my life, am I going to keep doing what I am doing or am I going to change" then don't change as we are struck or don't know how to change.

We can change our mood in a heartbeat. We can change our thinking, our mindsets, our income, our emotions, our conditioning and our paradigms. We can reprogramme ourselves to obtain happiness, health and wealth. It starts with changing our thinking which is done in a heartbeat then the mood follows. Those around us follow as well.

Our thoughts are energy that we cannot see, hear, touch, taste or smell in the physical form. Like attracts like so positive attracts positive and negative attracts negative. If you look for the negative in people you will find it the same goes for the positive if you look for it you'll find it.

I find life is better when I respond and do not react in any given situation, especially negative ones. I tend to look for the win, win solutions to any problem I may have, so everyone wins.

Objects start life in someone's mind, they have an idea and they see what it looks like, how it feels, the smell of it and if it's food or a drink what it tastes like. Then move into action they write it down, draw up plans, and make flow charts of how to get it in reality. This includes research and market research.

These people do not stop until their object is created and then they might want to sell it so the work continues with market research. A sofa or chair didn't just appear they are someone's brainchild!! They had the idea and they worked at bringing it to life just like James Dyson he made 5,127 prototypes of his vacuum cleaner before he was successful. He did not stop until he reached his goal then created more goals and expanded on his idea. He had the determination to succeed at producing his product.

1

Chapter 1 : Our Conditioning

Our conditioning starts when we are born and carries on until we die. Conditioning is more prominent when we are children growing up.

This is when we don't have the option of which schools we go to, this option is down to our Parents/Guardians as we are growing up.

This is because we are not aware that we are being conditioned. We are conditioned by those we hang around with mostly our Parents, Teachers, TV, Social Media, friends and their family and friends.

We don't know this unless we are told about it and only then can we change who we hang around with. There are many layers to our conditioning.

Conditioning is part of our subconscious that is wide open at birth, what we are told by those around us is our conditioning.

We believe what they say is true which goes into our subconscious and then becomes the way we think for the rest of our lives. Unless we are willing to change it and be made aware of it.

Becoming aware of our conditioning is when we start to take notice of the world around us or we get fed up with living the way we are living and seriously want to change that and so we go searching for a way to change.

I was told growing up I would never make it as an author, which is what I wanted to become. I was told my handwriting was rubbish along with English, and English literature and my grammar was way below standard. So I would never make it, I believed them for nearly 30 years now look at me.

We believe our friends and family are telling us the truth as we trust them and we have no reason to suspect them of telling us lies.

As children, our minds are wide open for teachings and lessons and the fact we don't know any different to what people tell us, we accept what is being told is gospel and literal. Like if you pull that face long enough it will stick like it, Don't be scared of thunder, it's only God moving his furniture.

Until we recognise that we have been conditioned to fit in with those around us we cannot change. You must know who you are and where you are before moving on to being able to change.

The first step in changing is to know that a change must happen otherwise you will be stuck in the same pattern until you die.

We can change the way we are thinking and feeling temporarily in a heartbeat but making it stick is another challenge.

This challenge to making it stick doesn't happen overnight it's a series of steps to happen over time and you'll only take them when you are 100% ready for it and not before.

If you force it, it will not stick so you must be 100% ready for a change to happen. In the following chapters, I have broken down the steps and explained each step. I am not guaranteeing success for you from this book as everyone is different.

But it gives you a head start. If it does not work after you read it and have reread it after several times then you are not ready for the change just yet and you need to look deeper inside of yourself.

I said earlier that conditioning has many layers. Conditioning is formed from habits, and also what we are told early on. We have picked up many different habits as we have grown up some good, some bad.

I have learned from the best Bob Proctor, Tony Robbins, Eric Worre and Lauren Brown. I have removed certain negative people from my life including those who have tried to put me down and control me.

I, myself will only watch TV shows that star those people who I look up to, who are doing what I want to do and earning the sort of money I want to earn and I am following them for those reasons.

Many moons ago I took the first step into changing my life, little did I know, I wasn't completely 100% ready for a change as much as I wanted it, but I never stopped believing that I could have it.

Only recently have I looked back over my life and seen what I have done and what I have overcome and when I did them. I have closely looked at each part of my life and seen the chain of events.

When I believed something was going to happen, it did happen the way I imagined it would. When I was so focused on something and believing in myself to accomplish a goal I did it even with people putting me down and not believing in me that I would do it. I went and done it, I achieved that goal and I was proud I had accomplished it.

I did not realise then I was in charge of my own destiny, I say this everyone is in charge of their own destiny. You create your own path with your mind, you have the power to do so.

I can only speak from my own experiences and what I have learned from the best in the business and that have been doing it for years and made it work for them. So changing our mindsets, and our conditioning is not an overnight thing it can take months and years to change it.

The first step is knowing and be willing to change your conditioning for the better, your destiny is out there.

Paradigms as I understand them are habits and loads of habits piled on top of one another, and these habits are our behavioural habits that can either help us or hinder us to get what we want.

Something I have learned from Bob Proctor is how to change a paradigm, one step is to recognise our habitual behaviour and that it is part of our paradigm and this is part of our conditioning.

Once you see a habit or thought pop up that you don't want you can tell it to do one and that it is no longer welcome here. Or if you know the paradigms that are holding you back you can always write them down on a piece of paper then safely burn that piece of paper and say goodbye to that old paradigm you are no longer welcome here.

Once that has gone you should feel much lighter and can replace it with a paradigm that will help you reach your goal(s). I will keep mentioning Bob Proctor though out this book as he was a great mentor, and I can still hear him as write giving me guidance and advice whenever I need it. Even though Bob is now the world of spirit he will never stop mentoring me.

I follow Bob on YouTube and his website including on Facebook. He was a big part of my life and one of many who helped turn my life around.

Going to school can teach you all sorts of stuff and that is just gaining knowledge but what they don't teach us is how to use it or how to earn money. Nor do they teach about paradigms and how to go about changing them. We end up with our minds wide open for all sorts of junk to fly in throughout our whole lives.

What do you think about when I mention the word goals? I have a whole chapter on this later on, but for now, what do you think about your goals?

What did school teach you? what courses have you taken? What have you learned from your time on this planet so far? Are you working to live or live to work?

Getting out of our comfort zone is another challenge to take on, and all this can be overwhelming for people, I suggest when you start to feel overwhelmed take a step back just for a moment or two and gather your thoughts before carrying on. If still overwhelmed take an even longer break but always come back and push yourself out of your comfort zone that way you will grow and expand in ways you would never have imagined.

It's hard at first but as go it gets easier and easier, there are a few tips and tricks along the way that I too have picked up and would like to share them with you in this book.

I am learning new tips and tricks every day from my mentors as I am on the six minutes to success course with Bob. I watch the little videos every day and every time I watch one I learn something new.

Something I have learned lots from Bob but from the Universe as well, in 2019 either at the start or around June time I had a reading from a friend. She told me that I am destined for big things, I'm not telling you any more of that reading as it is private.

In 2020/21 I had a crow fly into my living room window, the dam thing kept doing it. When I thought it had finished it had only flown around flat to the kitchen window and started attacking that window.

This crow kept doing it, which it was winding Edith up (my dog). I was frightened, to say the least. I reached out to two of my friends that are Spiritual, one is the one that gave me a reading previously and the other I go to for a hot stone massage and some reiki healing. They had told me that it is nothing to be frightened of and in fact that it is a good omen and that it is a sign of me going through a transitional period.

I asked how do I get it to stop and how long do I have to put up with this crow attacking my windows. I was advised to ask the universe a question and offer bread/food then say thank you for visiting me.

I did so for a couple of days, and after 3 days of doing that the crow disappeared and stopped attacking the windows. So I got the message loud and clear that I am moving in the right direction, the direction I want to go in. Do you know what it feels pretty goddam good. Sorry for my swearing but after what I have been through in the past, you would not blame me for doing so. That is a little something I have learned from the universe.

Sorry I went off there on a bit of a tangent there any way moving on as we learn new habits old habits disappear as there is no room for them. The way we learn new habits is through repetition, it takes 21 days to form a new habit.

One new habit I got very recently which happened a couple of years ago was brushing my teeth every day because as a youngster I was a rebel and didn't like brushing my teeth, I hated it so I made up excuses for why I never did it. I didn't understand then why it was so important to brush your teeth I just never got it, up until recently. Of course, I have brushed my teeth in all my years but it wasn't a habit that never formed when I was growing up.

It was only when I started having major problems with my teeth during the pandemic did the habit start to form. I find myself when I take my dog out for a walk in the morning I'll remember to brush my teeth then before I walk out the door with her, if I wait until I come back I won't brush my teeth as I will forget as I have other things on my mind.

That habit did take 21 days to form and I had to find out how I could find the time to brush my teeth every day without forgetting, and through the pain, I found it lol. I'm not saying you have to go through pain to find out the good habits, it is just one way of many.

2

Chapter 2 : Believing in something

Believing in something, I am not talking about religion here nor am I preaching about some God or Goddess. In order for us to change, we must believe we can change. Belief starts on the inside, if you believe something will happen it will happen. As you think about it more and more, the more it will come. If you believe and expect bills to come through the mail it will do, if you believe and expect cheques to come through the post, they will do. Whatever we think about and believe and expect things to happen guess what they are going to happen.

Just before I got pregnant with my daughter I believed that me and my brother's girlfriend at the time would be pregnant at the same time I had only joked about it to start with. I even fantasised a little about it, Imagining how people would react to the news if we were to be pregnant at the same time. You know what it became a reality no joke.

Whatever I imagined myself doing has become a reality at some point. Like driving and passing my driving test, I imagined myself driving a red Ford Fiesta down the road with my mom sitting beside me which became a reality. At the time I was broke living on next to nothing and only just scraping by, and not really being able to afford a car and keep it on the road but here I was driving my car that was fully legal and above board. What I'm trying to say is in order for something to happen you must believe it first.

We all believe in something, those that say seeing is believing are not believing at all I'll cover this in the next chapter.

You must believe something wholeheartedly with all of your faith before anything happens. The more powerful the belief, the stronger feelings the quicker it happens, but understand this.

The universe hears you, all of your thoughts. So the stronger the thought the better so be careful of what you wish for!! As the universe hears your wish and will grant it. I say be careful what you wish for because what you give out you will get back threefold. A little side note there is usually a time delay and thank goodness there is!!

You wouldn't want to be looking at an elephant and then thinking about that elephant and then it's coming through your living room wall! Yes, some of what I saying has been said in the movie "The Secret".

If you haven't watched the movie "The Secret" I highly recommend that you do and also "Dare to Dream" both are good movies.

Here I am going off my personal experiences and what I learned from Bob Proctor and what I have learned from those two movies. There are countless other movies with hidden messages that relate to everyday life and the Law of Attraction including the principles of the Law of Attraction.

I did not understand it at first but now I do and I'm putting it all into practice. I have looked back over my life and analysed all the moments I can remember which I have put in my previous book "Ups and Downs of Life" there are bits I have missed out of that some on purpose and others not, but I know the universe was ready for that book.

I believed as I was growing up I would be an author even though I had no clue what genre I was going to write I knew deep down that I would be helping people in some way and now here am I writing my second book and have so many more in the pipeline.

Now the ideas keep flowing to me of what I could write about, 7 years ago I had no clue. I didn't even have a business I was just drifting through life as Bob would put it.

Now I have that spark there is no putting it out. So believe in something and get passionate about it, focus on it 100% no one can take your dreams away from you unless you let them.

I say this only you are in charge of your destiny no-one else is. I too have let other people control me, I have taken the reigns back. If I can do it so can you.

Have the belief within you that you can do it, the power is there. I have the belief that you can do whatever you want to do. It comes from within.

I do a lot of reading always learning something new, when you stop learning, you are dead inside. Some people may not like this as it's the truth and sometimes the truth hurts and they don't want to admit it to themselves.

I don't care what you believe in whether it is a God or Goddess it's the same energy to me. Some call it God, some call it a Goddess, some call it Source, some like me call it the universe, it's universal energy it's the same stuff whatever you wish to call it.

Before I started dating my late husband back in 2012, and I went on to this dating website I believed that I would meet a great guy and be married to him within a 2-year time frame. I believed it wholeheartedly and will all my soul, especially when I did meet my late husband Matthew and I started talking to him. We became friends on Facebook and started growing closer.

I believed him and me were meant to be a couple before we did become a couple. He went off with someone else. I can't blame him as that is what I did before we had our first date in March 2012. I still firmly believed after our first date we were meant to be, Matthew didn't believe it at first. I went off with this other chap just after the new year, and Matthew went off with another woman in March.

I and Matthew got together in May after this other woman told Matthew she did not love him after he had said "I love you" to her. It was the start of May when Matthew came crawling back to me.

We hit it off on our second date and two years later we were married. What I didn't see coming was my unfortunate loss of Matthew four days after the wedding, we didn't believe strongly enough that he was gonna live for a few more years after the wedding and the big C got him.

Even though I did believe wholeheartedly that I would be married within a two-year time frame what I failed on was the rest of our lives together as a couple I see that now.

I am learning from my mistakes and I will probably keep learning from them and I will never stop learning for as long as I live.

Yes I maybe a spiritualist but I am not above the Law of anything, Yes I believe in the hereafter and I do believe my husband to be a spirit now. I say "we are spirits having a human experience" not the other way around.

Life is full of lessons we may not know at the time but we do learn eventually. Sometimes we just have to live our best life the best we can and believe in something as we all do. Doesn't matter what it is we all believe something.

Believing in something is a natural law, we all do it, and it is only natural. In order to change our mindsets and what we believe is no easy task as I have mentioned in the previous chapter. I will keep mentioning it as it is important. Repetition is key.

You will find me repeating information throughout this book as repetition is key along with others. I too am still learning as I write this book and I started writing this book during the pandemic, I did not let it affect me, I carried on as normally as I could within the law of us humans (What the government says is the law or be put in jail for breaking the law)

Absorb this book then I suggest you reread it, to get even more benefit from it and my life experiences in 'Ups and Downs of Life' the more you learn about this stuff the more it will sink in and will affect your life in a good way.

Believing is part of faith which I will cover in another Chapter. I too have gone to a Christian church and believed in God but now I know God is the universe and is universal energy that runs through us all.

I know this will upset some people but I am just speaking the truth, As I have said there are many gods and goddesses along with demons and different animals and creatures which all blend in with their surroundings but us, no we don't blend in at all.

Whatever you believe is the truth for you, maybe it was the way you were brought up with your friends and family. What you were taught in school. What your parents believe in and it is passed on to you.

I always say life is what you make it and that cannot be further from the truth that it is truth. We can choose what we believe in, no one else has that power over us unless we let them.

All my life I have been sort of a rebel, not doing what I am told and how to do stuff I rebelled against some rules, and I have tried not to let other people tell me what to do and when to do it. What I have let them do is control how I feel. I am not letting that happen anymore I am in control of the way I feel, I choose the way I feel.

This is one of the reasons why I love being a published Author I can choose when I write and when the mood takes me. Then I am in charge of what I earn and no-one else has a say. I love being self-employed and working from home I get to spend time with family and other commitments like volunteering for The Max and George Trust and Canal and River Trust.

I believe, I am in charge of how I feel and my life and so it must be true. So whatever you believe is the truth, your subconscious has no way of rejecting anything you tell it from your conscious. Your conscious has the ability to accept or reject.

If you really truly believe that you will be rich guess what that is the truth as you believe it. If you believe you will always suffer and be in pain, guess what that is the truth you will as you put yourself there, more on this in another chapter.

Life is confusing so can this book be, if you believe it to be, I will try and keep it simple as I can for everyone.

When I first came across 'Think and grow rich' it was an audible book it pushed me way out of my comfort zone and I hated what it was saying, but now I'm understanding it more because Bob has broken it down for us.

You need a lot of patience and understanding in order for this to work for you and other people, Some people will call you crazy for believing in it. I too have been called crazy but as I have said previously I have looked over my life and analysed it, Seen where I believed in things and believed they would happen and they did, all because I believed and felt that they would come true.

The next Chapter is about seeing is not believing!! Intrigued? Read on then.

3

Chapter 3 : Seeing is not believing

Seeing is not believing at all, as mentioned in the previous chapter. Seeing is not believing because the object has already manifested in reality. Believing is to believe that something is not in reality yet or something you cannot see, hear, smell, touch or taste.

Put it this way I believe in spirits and the afterlife, I also believe everyone is capable of doing what they want to do as long as it's positive and in no way meant to hurt anyone else. You have to have purely good intentions.

Believing in the unknown is a question of faith. Seeing what is in front of you is not believing, when you say, you believe what is in front of you, you have no faith, you are thinking negatively with your logical brain.

That is fine if you just want to drift through life aimlessly and have no ambitions. You are entitled to your opinion and so is everyone else, but don't bring those around you that do have ambitions and high hopes for the future down.

If you are ambitious and have high goals then read on. I say believe in the unknown, say if you were driving a car at night in a thick fog all you can see is 10 meters in front of you, you know the road is still there just beyond the fog so you keep driving and you'll get to your destination, even though you cannot see it for the fog that is belief in the unknown.

Those that say seeing is believing have no vision and are stuck, rooted to the spot as they cannot see beyond the fog because they only believe what they can see. They will only move forward when the fog is lifted as then they see what is around them. In my book, this is having no faith, no belief and you won't go anywhere.

Say you get in your car and you drive from your home town to the next town which is some 10 miles away, you know that town is there but you cannot see it unless you are standing on a very high hilltop.

You can not see it while driving but you know it's there and you know the way. Even if you didn't know the way you would still drive as there will be signs pointing in that direction so you have faith you can get there, even if you did, unfortunately, get lost there will be someone who does know the way and you can ask for directions. Have faith and belief within yourself.

It took me a long time and a lot of devotion to retrain my mind to think about believing in the unseen in the material world, I have always believed in life after death though I cannot see the spirits around me. I have always believed they were there just out of eyeshot.

I was brought up with my mom's boyfriend who kept saying 'I'll believe it when I see it' which that, did have an impact on my life that it became one of my paradigms which is in conflict with me being a spiritualist, I believe in the unknown even more so now than I ever was growing up.

After my husband's passing which knocked the wind out of my sails for about 7 years and I didn't know about paradigms and the law of attraction and the law of vibration until I came across Tony Robbins, Frazer Brooks and Eric Worre on Facebook in 2018.

I did start doing affirmations and my belief in the unknown began to grow again never mind what my friends and family said to me at the time if it was negative. I was just pushing their belief systems and they did not like it, so they rebelled against me and I started pushing them away and went for positive people instead of the negative.

I am still learning all about it and my belief in the unknown has grown so big, that I can believe anything can happen and it does.

I believed good things are happening and I see them happening but the world is so focused on the bad they cannot see a way of out it, and that's all they see is happening. So time to believe in the unknown and become positive, good things are happening and it starts from within you.

I do affirmations every morning and as I believe it is true so does my subconscious which is then changing the way I think, feel, and respond to everything that is going on around me.

Believing in the unknown and what we truly desire within our hearts will come to pass, so be careful of your thoughts and your thought patterns as they can and will turn around and bite you in the ass if you are not careful I, myself have been there and done that and learnt from it.

Whatever you give out comes back threefold. I now choose to respond instead of reacting. There are times when I still react instead of responding that's just my nature being an Arian and having a little bit of Scottish blood in me, I prefer to respond and not react and keep calm lol.

I can even spot when I am about to react and snap at people, like the other day I got really fed up and frustrated at all my electrical gadgets and all the people coming at me at once, I choose not to snap at anyone and I walked away, I stood in my kitchen alone taking slow deep breathes to calm myself down. So that way I can think clearly and respond better.

Even though I have entitled this chapter Seeing is not believing I have gone way off course, I have added about what we send out unknowingly. This is something I get very passionate about and can ramble on and on and on about it, I too have done it but now I am becoming aware of what I send out, and that is changing my paradigms, my behaviours, my thoughts and my mindset which leads ultimately changing my autopilot.

Right back to this chapter in question seeing is not believing. As I have mentioned I believe in the Spiritual world, I know spirits exist I can feel them around me and on occasion I can hear them, especially in the morning when I am not quite awake, but just coming around from my sleep.

I believe the universe is always there, and it is always listening to your every thought, like what they say in the movie 'The Secret'.

I have a question for you do believe in magnets and forces? Can you see the forces that surround a magnet? Can you see what the forces are doing? Can you see the forces of the magnet pulling metal towards it?

No, you can not see the forces taking place, so you must believe that they working but cannot see them working. If you are struggling with this concept of seeing is not believing then think of magnets and sonar, they both have invisible forces we cannot see with our eyes, yet they are there.

If you believe something exists then it exists whether in your mind or in reality it exists somewhere, If you can hold an object in your mind, you can hold it in your hand. If you can go somewhere in your mind, you can go there physically.

You must know that there is a gestation period for it just like everything in this world. Understand this you must plant the seed in your mind and water it every day, think about it every day use your imagination, and feel as if you already have it, what does that feel like? do this every day.

Soon It becomes you and your body will move into action to attract what it is you want and do. Then you have it in reality. How does that feel? One thing we do not know is the gestation period, it could be a day, a week, a month or even a year, we just cannot put a time frame on it.

Gonna go off track, here again, I know I have already gone off track but hear me out this is the last bit to this chapter and I might come back to it in a later chapter.

Going on faith, and belief is just one small step to a bigger operation in order to change our autopilot, I have heard people say life is what you make it. I for one never really got that until quite recently as I have become more aware of the laws around me and their vibrations. I'll talk about this in another chapter.

I have been experimenting with manifesting recently too, using meditation and affirmations, I'm starting to use these more often as it is a way of calming down and focusing again I talk about this in another chapter.

Back to seeing is not believing, when I was growing up I had it drummed into me by my mom's boyfriend "I'll believe it when I see it" as I have already mentioned and I did mention just now I have been experimenting with the law of attraction and manifesting.

What I did was, try the theory out of the "I'll believe it when I see it" approach and guess what things that I wanted turned very soar, things turned in the opposite direction. Instead of positive and all things light, they turned negative and dark. So my depression was seeping back, that's including a lack of energy.

All I wanted to do was play games and watch TV in bed and not talk to anyone, I was not even writing, I couldn't face it. I even put off my training in Spear and got behind on my coursework with the writer's bureau.

Now as I live on my own with my dog I had to give myself a kick up the backside to get moving, including making motivational posters and putting them up in front of me.

During this experiment, my YouTube channel was falling at the wayside as well with the views, likes and subscriptions going down. That is when I decided it was time to end the experiment and go back to the positive vibes instead.

Once I did that, things were back on the up. So I can say with a hand on my heart that the experiment was I success as I learned from it and can share it with you. So I can say " Seeing is not believing". I have learnt a lesson and a valuable one at that.

And I did it consciously, I knew I could reverse it at any time and I proved it to myself and I will talk about it later. The reason why I mention this stuff now and again is that repetition is key to learning.

Repetition is the way we have always learned, it's how habits are formed and our habits control us. We can change our habits and autopilots which will take time but is doable.

The next chapter is about happiness, happiness comes from within and not the outside world and its material objects. We all fall into that trap!! I too have fallen for it. I have found what makes me happy, my heart and soul sing with joy.

Happiness is a key to success, I suggest you read on to find the other keys to success, I will try to keep it as simple as I can, I cannot make any promises of course as that is not me, I don't make promises I cannot keep.

Don't forget repetition is key to learning, it takes 21 days for new habits to form. I suggest you figure out what habits are holding you back and keeping you from moving on and on that note we will move on to the next chapter.

4

Chapter 4 : Happiness within

Happiness comes from within, not from the outside world which is a reflection of what is going on, on the inside. Our thoughts and processes are shown on the outside it is our feelings and what we put into our bodies including our mindsets.

We have to think about what truly makes us happy, and what do we want to do in life. What do we desire, our hearts desires? What do we want out of life?

Who do we want to spend our life with? What makes us feel loved and wanted? Is it time for self-reflection/personnel development?

What are our goals do they reflect what our hearts want? Are you in harmony with your goal(s)

Even Celebrities have goals and needs just like you and me. They are human too. They have found happiness within themselves and believed in themselves and everything else I am talking about, they too like shiny things. Most of them try to improve themselves to make themselves even better.

As in my previous book we all have ups and downs in life. Without the downs, we wouldn't know what the ups are. There is a balance to everything, A natural law like the law of gravity, we know it exists but we cannot see it.

So what is happiness to you? Me, I like a lot of things, I love walking on the beach watching the tide roll in and out, or sitting in my office writing books for entertainment and to teach others, being an inspiration that is my bliss.

I love walking my dog on the beach at sunset knowing I have made a difference to someone's life for the better and improving my own life at the same time by learning something new.

Happiness can be anything positive and it does come from within, within your heart and soul.

Too often are we looking at the negative, the negative side of life, when there is so much positive in the world. You don't have to be obnoxiously happy, but be at peace which is still happiness. There are lots of happy things around, you could be happy going to the pub and having a drink and meal out with friends and family or a night in, in front of the TV cuddling on the sofa.

Whatever makes you happy do it. I have fallen into that unhappy trap too. Now I listen to music or watch some comedy on TV. I sometimes have a dance around the flat to cheer myself up before now I even have posters to motivate me dotted around the flat, so when I am not at my best and feel like throwing in the towel I just look and read all the posters I have created, I even have taken inspiration from the YouTube channel Proctor Gallagher Institute. I remind myself what I love doing and what I want out of life.

Or I try and talk to my boyfriend or my close friends they seem to help me get back my happiness but advertently it comes from within.

Material items can make you happy for a short period of time, Happiness, as I have said not long ago, comes from within not the outside world. I think we are happiest when we are spending time with friends and family, enjoying each other's company, I know I do. Sometimes just meditating makes me happy and relaxed.

Happiness within can be found in many ways like meditating and asking for guidance. Experimenting, trying new things. Find a quiet place to sit and relax to connect with your higher self I know this sounds kinda hippie, new Agey thing but it's not, it is part of the secret and it has been going on since the dawn of time.

We as humans are meant to be happy, Yes I know there are bad and rough times but remember the bad times are just a phase and the good, better times are on their way. Keep positive even on bad days.

I have health issues at the moment but I am not going to let that pull me down, some days I get depressed and I remind I am tired and that is why I am feeling that way, I either go to sleep if its late at night or put some upbeat 80's tunes on or some comedy to cheer me up until I go to bed.

Another way of cheering myself up is thinking of how I would feel if I had x, y, and z. How am I going to feel when I reach one of my goals that I have been working on?

I will use my imagination and fantasise about doing what I love in the here and now, I imagine how people respond and react when they see me, or talk to me. I allow all positive comments and remove the negative ones.

A little tip for you, when you notice a negative thought or emotion tell it "get out of here you are not welcome" and it goes, then replace it with a positive thought or emotion.

As we go through this book you should start to become more aware of your surroundings and vibrations. I'll come to this later in the book.

If I catch myself saying to myself "I don't feel well, I'm tired" I start doing a chant which is repeating the same line over, and over and over again until I feel better and happy. This line I say to myself is 'I am happy, healthy and wealthy'.

This usually happens in the morning not long after I wake up so I pull myself together and start the day happy and cheerful. Then I'm ready to take on the day and work on my social media including writing my books.

Gone off track slightly there as I do, as you can see where my passion is, laugh out loud. Back to it, happiness is different for everyone all you have to do is find it and things will start to slot into place.

One of the keys to happiness is finding what you love, I found that right here it was in front of me the whole time, I couldn't see it for looking until I was so relaxed one day then I asked myself what is it that I love doing and dawned on me that I love writing, doesn't matter what it is about.

If I have a pen and paper in my hand I will start writing all sorts, whatever is in my head at the time, it's like a pensive from the world of Harry Potter if you have ever seen or read the books you'll know what I'm on about.

Things just come pouring out of me, like talking to the camera on my YouTube channel when I do my vlogs, I do ramble on. I wasn't like that at the start of doing the vlogs, I was camera shy. I pushed myself out of my comfort zone in order to grow and share myself with the world like I did with my first book.

One of many reasons why I did that was to help others that are going through what I went through, as I have heard that too many people are not making it out of depression and continue on the downward spiral until their ultimate end.

I have been there, and got the t-shirt. I found my way out with the help of family and friends. It is not a nice place to be in so I wanted to help other people and I hear that it has helped, it fills my heart and soul with joy. As that is my happiness, to be helping others, it is my go-to place.

Everyday I think of all the people I have helped and going to help, that makes me happy. I am filled with joy and that puts my vibration really high I'll talk about vibrations in another chapter, I have made a whole chapter on it. I will keep coming back to vibrations as it is a key to success and vitally important.

There are sad times and there are happy times. Just remember out of the sad comes happy times. Once I was invited to the London book fair which would of cost me nearly £2000 to go but I couldn't see myself raising the funds in time. I did think to myself that there is something bigger and better coming my way even though I was gutted I couldn't make it. I kept thinking that there is something bigger and better in store for me.

So when times are bad and there's something you want like going to a concert you are unable to remember there will be something bigger and better coming along for you. I know this sounds a bit cliche but always look on the brighter side of life, yes I know that is the title of an old song. The fact of the matter is that there is always a positive side to things even when things look bleak.

What's in the past stays in the past, I came across a little note the other day while going through a box of Neals Yard Remedies Organic stationery, it wasn't in my handwriting it looks like my step-sister's handwriting but she wouldn't have written anything like this 'write a letter of forgiveness for an apology you'll never get'.

This to me is letting go of those that have hurt me and the negative energy I am holding on to, which is stopping me from loving life and living it to the max. That energy is stopping me from doing what I want to do with my life.

When I visualise that I have forgiven those that have hurt me and I'm letting go of the negative energy, I feel a lot happier and at peace with myself, That is me letting love in to heal me on all levels.

I have let people get the better of me for too long and I have let them control how I feel, I have had a lot of negative energy to deal with and let go of over the past few years and I will continue to improve myself as I still some to get rid of.

I am no longer letting other people control me and my feelings, and I choose to let positive energy in, I tell myself I am respected and loved by many never mind the haters as there will always be haters and bullies, so I choose to get on with my life and help those that genuinely want and need help if I can provide it.

Be at peace within yourself, and everything else falls into place. Be happy with what you are doing if you are not happy then change it. It is OK to be happy with yourself. Changing your habit to something that you love is easy, if it is a good habit but don't like it will take longer to change than a good habit that you love. It usually takes 21 days to change a habit.

It has taken awhile for me to start loving myself after my husband's passing but I am finally getting there with the help of YouTube channels, family and friends. Also it maybe beneficial to keep negative people at arm's length and start hanging around with positive people.

Positive people that you hang around with will impact your life in many ways, you will start to see the positive side of life and internally you'll be happier, then that turns into a positive vibration and you'll be able to attract what you want but this is just one step with many other steps to attract what you want.

The world is your oyster, it's up to you what you make it. The goals I have are quite big and very ambitious, it may take me a year or more to reach them. I don't how I'm going to get there or how long it is going to take me to get there but I will get there.

5

Chapter 5 : The Mind

The Mind is not part of the brain like most people think it is. The mind is a lot bigger than the brain and more powerful than you think, along with the subconscious it cannot be seen so we don't have an image for it, I quote Bob Proctor here. He has many slides and explains this concept better than me at this moment as I am still studying and will do until I pass over to the other side.

The mind can either make you or break you, it really does depend on how you were brought up. This chapter is looking at the mindset and the mind.

The mind is very powerful, it can only accept what you feed it, or put it another way what you plant in it. we have more than 6,000 thoughts in a single day we may not realise this fact and we can not govern all 6,000 thoughts a day.

So enter the autopilot which can govern over 6,000 thoughts a day, That is what this book is really about 'How we manifest - Changing our Autopilot' that seems scary to some and puts people on the back foot but that is in itself is our autopilot which is rejecting that thought of change or possible change.

Change scares some people which is basically a fear that we will come to in our next chapter.

The subconscious mind doesn't have the ability to reject. It just accepts what was already has been planted.

The Autopilot(paradigms) is a group of habits that we have gotten into for one reason or another. In order to change our autopilot, we have to change our habits. Oh dear, I've gone off track again lol.

Bear with me here a moment, this is what I have learnt from Bob Proctor. Paradigms/Autopilot is habitual behaviour and all behaviour is habitual which can be changed, sorry just had to get that off my mind!

The mind has the power to change our autopilot, it has the power to change the vibration we are in like night and day. I have done a whole chapter on this further on in the book.

Before I started writing this book, my mindset was of poverty I kept thinking of lack of money which I didn't realise I was doing, up until quite recently. My thoughts were I want that but I cannot afford it, I don't have the money. I kept doing this all the time and I wasn't getting anywhere, money was just slipping through my fingers like water.

I'm changing the way I think, it's a slow process, as I identify the bad habitual behaviour and change it to good habitual behaviour, the way I think has even changed. I look back over the past week or month and I see the change in myself.

Just the other day I found out that my attitude was bad, I did not like a lot of things and my attitude towards others was horrible, so that's now being changed the more I see me changing and how it's affecting me, I want to help others to do the same that's if they want to change that is.

As I understand all this I am changing my mindset and the way I treat others. My heart may have been in the right place but my attitude was quite another, I see that now. Losing my husband really did knock the wind out of my sails.

Back to the chapter in question. The mind is a very powerful object yet we cannot see it. It can make dreams into reality. Use the mind to create ideas and then plant them in your subconscious garden and water daily.

The conscious mind has the ability to reject stuff and accept stuff, the mind has lots of areas working all at the same time most of which are on autopilot all the time. Like Memory, Reason, Perception, the will, how we come to decisions, our thoughts and our imagination all of which has a chapter in this book.

What else can I say on the mind? Well, it has the ability to control levels of pain. Some women can give birth without pain relief because in their mind childbirth is not painful, and then you have others who need all the pain relief medication you can give them because in their mind childbirth is very painful.

Take going to the dentist and you need a tooth removing, it will be as painful as you think it is. Unless you can go to a place in your mind where there is no pain whatsoever and it will be all over before you know it.

Another example is food if your mind is on doing something and you are not thinking of food you will not be hungry. The minute someone mentions food your mind instantly jumps onto the food thought and then you realise you are hungry. People have missed meals because they were not thinking about food at the time. Now I'm thinking about food I'm hungry because I am talking about it.

So as I keep mentioning the mind is powerful and it controls most of our bodily functions. You're probably thinking, so how do I change my mindset, We change the mindset by changing our habitual behaviours.

I have in this book little hints and tips for doing so. If you want it badly enough you will change it and find the habitual behaviours that are no longer serving you get rid and change them for the better.

Writing this book is also teaching me at the same time as I am understanding it as I write and go along so it's stretching my mind to new concepts and understand it better as I have Bob Proctor in my mind teaching me and helping me to help you, like I said I will always study this subject until I pass on over to the other side.

It is my passion to write and help others where I can. I am a spiritualist and sensitive to the spiritual world so it's easy for me to channel Bob Proctor and keep learning from him.

Bob Proctor did this for over 60 years and I will keep going back to his teachings and as the more I write, the more I understand it. I then put it in this book as I have not come across a book that puts the secret in plain language for the UK that is for dummies like me, I used to be like a dummie until I asked for spiritual assistance.

As I have mentioned before I got confused by the movie 'the secret' and learning this 'The law of attraction' business but it fascinated me enough to keep learning and to see what I was doing wrong and where I was going wrong.

Until I looked through my life of Ups and Downs, I didn't understand one little bit. Now writing this book is teaching me how to do it as I learn more I write more and understand it.

I even re-read Bob Proctors' books which they are slowly changing my mindset for the better. I am learning more about the mind and how powerful it really is not just from Bob but from other people too.

I love learning about it I find it all fascinating, I have mentioned that I have run an experiment and learnt from it, and now I'm back on the up again, yet again I have gone way off track in trying to explain the mind.

Whatever is going through my mind I seem to write it out here as if on autopilot lol.

The mind can help you with different things in life especially when you decide to meditate on an idea, I will talk about meditation in another chapter in this book. I love meditation finding the time to meditate can be difficult at times as I live by myself and only my dog for company. I have found time when to meditate daily. More on this in another chapter.

Learning new habits isn't easy as I for one do have one to break which is watching too many YouTube channels and finding new ones to watch, which is not paying me to do so and I get behind on my writing and my online courses and all the things I have to do.

So it is important to keep focused and the mind can help you do that, and kick the old habits that are no longer serving you, I have plenty of bad habits to get rid of. You can only change one to two habits at a time. It takes 21 days to change a habit.

One habit I must change is time management it needs improving, as much as I love writing and writing this book, it's pushing my mind to change so I have part of my mind not wanting to do this and the other that wants to do it.

When I open this book to write, I just start writing. It's like an addiction that's when I found my passion for writing. Never mind what I am writing about then I just get into the zone of writing and what I am writing about.

Then it just flows out of me as if I know what I'm writing about, occasionally I miss words as my mind is going so fast with the words my hands cannot keep up. I do not know if this is the same for all authors, especially for this genre.

But it is getting easier to do as I learn and teach it to you. I do have to keep pausing and checking what I have written. I am developing my mind and changing the way I think about stuff, my mind is being stretched for the better, as I improve my life, I help you do the same.

I know some of this should be in the introduction, but I feel it is better and friendlier to add it to the chapters throughout the book.

Then that way you are more comfortable and can relate to what I am saying. This is what I find when reading other books like this, and Bob's new book is very similar to what I am doing here.

As I go through the book I will be putting little stories in about myself and maybe you can relate to them and then it will help you understand this a little more.

The mind is very complex no robot can duplicate it. All of the emotions and the way we understand things. Each mind is as different as the next, but we are one conscious mind which I will get to later.

I love understanding how the mind works and how powerful it is. It can make anything real, it has the power to do so. If you hold it in your mind you can hold it for real, I love that saying from Bob Proctor.

The mind will even block out everything that is going on around you, Like I'm writing this and there are kids playing outside making a lot of noise but in my mind, there is no noise coming from outside as I concentrate on writing this piece and finishing this chapter, so I can get on the next chapter. I can only hear them when I lift my head out of the computer to have a breather.

The next chapter is overcoming your fears which I cannot wait to get on to, as I too have overcome many fears and want to share them with you guys. So what can I say other than time to move on to the next chapter, see you there and good luck. Hope you have learnt something from this chapter on the mind.

6

Chapter 6 : Overcome fears

Overcoming fears is a big thing. It is not easy to do. After my husband passed, I locked my heart up and never let anyone in for years. When I realised what I did I cried my heart out as I never let myself feel the pain of the loss of my husband as I feared that pain and didn't want to feel it. I buried my head in the sand so to speak. It is hard to let people back in as I was frightened of getting hurt again and I didn't want to feel that amount of pain again.

So I overcome that and let my heart out of its prison box slowly and gently and eventually letting love back in.

Some people say face your fears but if you don't what you are frightened of how can you face them?

I say if you don't know what they are then take a really good look inside yourself to find your fears then you can overcome them. It is different for everyone, how to overcome them. I usually do some meditation and ask for guidance on how to overcome my fear. To quote Sandy Gallagher and Bob Proctor "JUMP!! Wings will grow along the way".

There will be a lot of quotes from Sandy Gallagher and Bob Proctor. As I am new to this and very fresh at it. I understand enough of it to put it into simpler terms.

You may need to have a buddy for encouragement to help you, to overcome your fears and to have your back. It will get hard at times and you will want to give up and just live with that fear.

I didn't have that buddy just had myself as I wouldn't let anyone in or get too close as it was my fear of if I let someone get too close I'll only get hurt and get let down again and again.

So I had to do it myself if I wanted to change. It comes down to me to change and change my way of thinking.

Overcoming your fears comes down to your paradigms and behaviours. Paradigms are your autopilots, what you do on autopilot, without thinking. We all have them and they are not all bad, some no longer serve you and are holding you back from what you want to do. Some are based on fears. We do things automatically based on our fears which are habits we have picked up.

One thing you have to do is figure out what is holding you back and what your fears are and where have they come from before you can take the next step to overcoming them.

I had a fear of being in front of a camera or talking in public because of the fear of being judged, I got over that fear by writing my first book 'Ups and Downs of life' then I marketed that on Social media and then I got interviewed by Kate Delaney An author and radio show host over in America. Then eventually I started my YouTube channel at first I was nervous but I pushed myself out of my comfort zone and told myself that it would be ok as I had some stuff to share and not everyone reads.

My passion to share stuff was greater than the fear of the camera and I'm glad I did it as it has helped other people plus I can make money from it and promote my books and future books on there as well all part of the marketing strategy. If no knows about my books how can people buy them?

I have been frightened of Spiders and Snakes, I still am a little frightened but not as much as I used to be, as I'm getting an understanding of them. Sharks are another matter altogether as I try to understand them the great white will always frighten me thanks to that movie 'Jaws', I watched it when I was 7 and my big brother always teased and tormented me about it, so that's deep-rooted and going to take some getting over in which I am not ready for.

The fear of spiders is going, as just the other day there was a big spider in the bath and I would normally kill it by drowning it and sending it down the plug hole, but this time I didn't. I got a piece of cardboard and my Neal's Yard

Remedies Organic travel mug, I put the mug over the top of him/her and slid the piece of cardboard underneath him/her.

I could feel the spider moving around as walked to the balcony, my heart was racing ten to a dozen, and my breathing was shallow. I pushed past that as it was in my heart not to kill this spider. With a big swooping action, I removed the piece of cardboard from underneath the spider and he/she went for a flying lesson over the balcony!

I haven't seen the spider since. So I am slowly overcoming my fear of spiders I could never of have done that before, I would of have just killed it in the bathtub. I pushed myself out of my comfort zone now I feel better for it. If I can do it so can you. It's amazing what you can do if you just put your mind to it.

Overcoming your fears is part of changing your mindset and Autopilot. Another fear I had and overcoming is the fear of spending money if I had money I'd have to spend it straight away and so I was pushing money away because every time I had any money I have to spend it whether I needed to or not and so wouldn't stick to me and I always ended up owing money.

Overcoming fears is a case of getting out of your comfort zone and growing as a person, as I have mentioned I was camera shy before doing my YouTube channel I did one video, then a couple of days later I did another, I did another video not long after and started to get addicted to it, then I decided that I would a video every single day no matter where I was.

I was getting over my camera shyness and making videos everyday, building my confidence in being in front of the camera. The reason for being camera shy was because of fear of being judged by everyone, and that came from being bullied in high school and so I didn't like being the centre of attention but now I do and cannot get enough of it lol.

I thought to myself if I want to be a famous author I have to get used to being the centre of attention. If I want to be a motivational speaker I have to get used to public speaking.

I may have gone on stage in front of 35,000 people in Germany back in 2019, Yes I was camera shy then, but I got carried away in the moment and I wasn't on stage alone there were loads of us on stage, you're talking about 50 of us altogether on that stage all at the same time.

I was frightened but I thought what hell these people are not going to see me again are they, so I just went for it. It felt great because I started the ball rolling on getting over that fear.

So yes like people say face your fear or other words get out of your comfort zone and grow, that is what we are here for to grow and expand, there is no other feeling like it, it is totally bliss.

I'm falling in love with doing it, the relief that comes afterwards puts you on cloud nine for days, because you are releasing a negative emotion which is being replaced by a positive emotion.

When I went over to Germany it was my first time out of the country on my own I was nervous, not about flying, I was going to another country on my own, and I wanted someone with me. Now I have done it once I can do it again and nothing is going to stop me. The power you get from overcoming your fears is beyond words.

As I write this chapter I can only be in front of the camera on my settee or in my bedroom come office, I was nervous when I created videos when my friend stopped over for the weekend and I felt as if I had to involve her in the video some way.

I pushed past that fear and just got on with it. Now I'm thinking of going a step further and making the videos outside with different people around. I may have to meditate about it before I do make videos outside and talking to my phone.

As I think about it, I have become aware of my breathing and I'm going dizzy, and feeling faint plus my hands are getting hot and sweaty, not a good look. It is my fear to overcome next if I am to grow and expand.

It is just sinking in that I already have a book published and the fact that I am a published Author now after so many people and teachers told me that I wouldn't become a published Author, so I was frightened of getting my first book published as in the back in my mind a little voice kept telling me that no one will read it and it's completely rubbish, no one wants to read that it's boring, who in God's green earth is going to read it?

I had help from Jobs22 and my good friend in Southampton, and they gave me the support I needed to get it published, I was making excuses for not publishing, and one of them was the lack of money. I soon found out that you don't need money to become a published Author.

Getting on the Radio with Kate Delaney yes I needed money for that, I was nervous about doing that interview but I got through it. I needed lots of hugs and support to get me through it.

Sometimes getting over fears, all we really need is that little reassurance that everything is going to ok and that there is nothing to fear and no one will judge us for doing so. It may upset some people because we're changing and they don't like that we are changing for the better, it forces them to change as well.

As I have said not long ago if you can overcome your fears, You'll be on cloud nine when you do. As the fact the realisation of becoming a published Author is sinking in, I'm on cloud nine and I am proud of myself, as I never thought I would be a published Author. All the obstacles that were in my way were just illusions that I made up in my mind.

I'll give you this advice go out there and be brave. Think about what are the positives of this action, and what happens if you don't do it. The scarier it is the greater the reward but please take care don't do anything silly and think you can take on a very poisonous snake you may not live to tell the tale.

If you thinking about doing anything dangerous get the proper training first, please for goodness sake lol. Our bodies are not invincible they do break along with emotions. This bit is only a warning. I am not telling anyone what to do lol.

Life is precious but exciting nonetheless. Yes, life is for living and yes it is too short for some. I love life and I am happy to be here.

Overcoming fears is just another challenge in life and getting over them is exhilarating, it makes you feel powerful alive! I love that feeling, it's like ecstasy, not that I have taken ecstasy but that feeling is addictive.

7

Chapter 7 : Love

Love is one of many keys to success and it is an important key to getting whatever it is you want. I have had anger, jealousy, rudeness, frustration, and all negative emotions running through me.

I have watched my favourite TV programmes and thought 'What do they possess that I do not? What makes them so special and so happy? I want that too, I had that happiness I want it back!! I was missing my husband, I wanted my husband back which is impossible as now he is in the spiritual world.

I realised they had love, support and positive people around them. I have to let love in, to become my happy, bubbly self again.

That is when I really started to follow Bob Proctor and make new positive friends but I always kept my guard up, but I learned to love again. I am starting to socialise better and I have a lot of learning to do. I am an introvert and have always been shy. As I found my love for writing, that's when I really got to grips with my first book 'Ups and Downs of Life' and got it published.

Things are on the up for me because now I look at the positive side of things now instead of the negative, and I am loving life.

When I met my late husband I was desperate for someone to love me for who I was. After having guidance from the spirit world and going to church for healing as I was in desperate need of healing really bad.

After several sessions of healing at Tamworth Spiritualist Church back in

2011, I started to love myself first and then the things around me including people. I have never really been a people person, as my upbringing was a negative one, which my mom nor any of my friends and family hadn't realised what they were doing at the time.

So after the healing, love and respect from people at the Spiritualist Church, I had a feeling or an urge to go on to a dating website as I knew I wasn't going to meet anyone decent enough for me in Tamworth and I will not take them seriously as I thought they were all a bunch of idiots in the Tamworth area they were just after a quickie, never mind who it was with.

I wanted something more, I wanted a relationship that had love and feelings etc. That's what I had found on this dating website, a loving relationship that was going somewhere.

In order for that to happen, I had to love myself first, and love the body I was in and not fight it. Let me tell you this love does not come from the outside world as we are brought up to believe.

Love comes from within before anyone else can love us the way we want them to love us. Love is a key to happiness, so we must set ourselves upon the frequency of love and everything on that frequency flows to us. This is something I have had to learn time, time and time again.

After studying the natural laws and the law of attraction and experiencing them first and I can say for definite that it works. I have come off the tracks loads of times, I have got back up, dusted myself off and put myself back on the tracks.

One thing I have done and still doing is becoming more aware of what I am doing. I am getting quicker and quicker at spotting when I am coming off the tracks and I am then able to adjust and put myself back on the tracks.

I do personnel development every single day without fail I have turned it into a habit. I am becoming more aware of my thoughts and my actions everyday.

In order to love myself everyday has been a challenge as when I was growing up I was put down about my weight, I was bullied about it at school and at home by my moms' boyfriend. He kept saying no one will ever love you, because you are so fat, untidy, and you are not pretty. No-one will love you and no-one will marry you, you are just too ugly.

That's why I needed spiritual healing. I picked up a little advice from somewhere I cannot remember where but a little birdie told me to look into the mirror everyday and tell yourself that you love yourself and you are pretty, as you say these things look into your eyes and into your pupils as they are the windows to your soul.

Doing what I just said, is doing an affirmation in the mirror and when you do, it feels wonderful. Without loving and respecting yourself first, you just will not get anywhere, you do all the actions necessary, it will not work without love and respect.

Love is a frequency as well as respect, if you give those out you get them back in return. I have made a few posters and put them around the flat, to help, motivate, inspire me, and get out of the bad habits I have created for myself.

They will not do anything without the feeling of love and respect for myself. I have learned whatever negative comments come my way will not hurt me unless I let them. I have way too much self-respect to let that happen.

I have learned to love and respect myself again, and let the negative people just walk on by as karma will take care of them. Let yourself breathe in the love and positive energy, and let out the negative with each breath I have done this many a time, and I felt better afterwards.

It feels like a big heavy weight has been lifted off your shoulders, the relief is love pouring in and filling your boots. If think everyone is out to get you and judge then they probably are but if you change your thinking to everyone loves you then they probably do.

Think lucky, and you'll be lucky but thinking will not do it on its own you have to add in emotions of love and belief. Think back over your life and look at the key moments in your life, when you were feeling lots of emotions whether it be happy or sad, what happened following those feelings of pure joy or sadness? Those things just did not happen by accident!

Everyone has love inside them, they have a passion for something. For me, it's writing just give me a pen and paper and I will write for hours and I'll even forget that I've made myself a cup of tea even though I am thirsty.

I'll always find something to write about even if it's utter rubbish!! I cannot help myself it is an addiction for me, it's like a drug, and deep down I know it can and will help someone.

Someone that I know is passionate about property, marketing including websites and everything that goes with it like all the tech. Some people maybe passionate about painting or drawing, and there are some who love trains. Each to their own I say. Who are we to judge?

Love is a very pleasant feeling it can also heal on all levels Spirit, mental and physical. Love is powerful and we all have it within us. Love comes in many forms, sometimes when we least expect it.

I was at a car festival (cougarfest a car club for the cougar car) when I met my present boyfriend, I was not expecting it, I just gave him a hug goodbye, like see ya later sort of hug, a friendly one! We exchanged phone numbers on the car club forum in a private chat because he was gonna give me a lift to the next car show as I was without any wheels to get there and I was not expecting it.

He even took me out for a meal, he was working his way into my heart that was broken and heavily locked away so it wouldn't get damaged again as I could not take any more pain or have it broken into a million pieces again I could not face going through that much pain again.

He did worm his way in eventually when I started opening myself up to let love in. I softened to his advances. And the rest is history as they say. I'll never forget my true love, my first husband, yes I still miss him and I will still shed tears for him as I miss him so much, as it still hurts but at least I have the love of my friends, family and my new boyfriend who is understanding and will be there for me, when I do my teary moments.

I know my first husband will not want me crying, he will want to move on and love life, and he will always be by my side. He will be there whenever I call. I love having love in my life.

In order for it to come to me, I have, had to love myself first for who I am and no one is going to change that except for me. I too have struggled with this concept and believe me it works.

When I am in a bad place, I do not just simply go on the phone, I use instant meditation and contact whoever I can think of at that time which is usually my boyfriend and within about 5 minutes or an hour or so he's reaching out to me and contacting me.

The reason why I say I'm contacting my boyfriend spiritually is because at the moment he lives over 250 miles away from me. He texts me to find out if I am ok, and will keep messaging me until I answer, and if I don't he'll ring me it always works.

Even though this book is tough to finish especially the writing goals to complete everyday is tough I am pushing myself to do it because I love the feeling of when I have reached my goal and I can give myself a pat on the back and give myself a little treat.

I am pushing myself out of my comfort zone in order to grow, and obviously, I love writing so the writing goals are getting easier, so I give myself little challenges to complete so I can grow.

We all have distractions in our lives me included, life can so get busy you can easily forget what you love doing, because of all of the demands we have on our daily lives. We let the outside world control us. Get back to what you love doing and create time for it.

Yes, I know life is a juggling act, especially for those that have families to take of including our pets as they are too family members. As I have been writing about my boyfriend he has messaged me to make sure I'm ok, even though he knows I'm busy writing this book.

And yes, I will go into mediation in the next chapter for those who are wondering. As this chapter comes to a close I am filled with bliss because I am close to finishing today's goal.

My suggestion for you is to give yourself little challenging goals everyday and when you complete them and go past the goalposts, the bliss and the love for yourself is beyond words. It gives you so much pride and it can bring you to tears especially if it's a big goal or achievement. Tears will flow with Joy.

Allow yourself to feel all of the love in the world and the universe. You will not regret it. I do not regret it one bit I love it. I allow it during meditation which I will get to next.

8

Chapter 8 : Meditation

Mediation helps us figure out what we want and calms us from the hustle and bustle of our daily lives.

We can calm ourselves and connect with the universe, and be at peace. We can balance our chakras and relax.

We can even get messages and pick up on spirits, we ask the universe for stuff that way too as well as in many other ways.

There is even instant meditation, which I have used to get a parking spot in a busy car park.

Meditation is a relaxation technique used by many people around the world, many people have heard about meditation but do not understand it or how it works.

We can use meditation for a number of reasons, I have mentioned but a few above. I'll get into how to do it in a minute.

At first, I know it can be difficult to get into a relaxed state enough for you to meditate properly.

The more you meditate easier it becomes as it is like a mental muscle that needs strengthening. Like all muscles the more you work them the stronger they become.

It also takes discipline to train your brain and mind to relax and relax the body and let yourself drift into relaxation. There are many guided meditations on YouTube and Mediation music.

There are even guides for beginners to explain mediation. I am not an expert in Meditation and Do not have a doctorate to say that I am an expert, I have taken a course in reiki healing from a reiki master but I am only level one.

So I can only advise, and explain to the best of my knowledge and my life experiences. Plus how I meditate. I am getting myself into a routine of meditating daily.

Here are a couple of YouTube channels to check out on manifesting and meditation: Meditation, Master Sri Akarshana, Kenneth Soares and Simply Hypnotic.

I will not put a guided Meditation here, just a simple relaxation technique for meditation.

Find somewhere to sit or lie down but keep your back straight so all your chakras are in alignment and connect and flow with each other. Do not cross your legs, ankles or arms as that hinders the flow of energy.

Make sure it is somewhere, where you will not be disturbed by outside noises, put your phone on 'do not disturb' mode or silent will do. Put some Meditation music on or a guided Meditation and follow what they are saying.

If you are just putting some Meditation music on which helps with relaxation then the next steps are for you. Plus it helps to keep you grounded we do not want to be flying off to the nether world lol or leaving your body open to anything that could be floating around, now I do not want to scare you but it has happened in the past, not to me but someone else. If you are frightened then go to a professional who teaches it and can guide you through it.

They can help keep you grounded and also sense vibrations so know who and what is floating around and of course, they have spiritual guides to help guide them to help you.

So I'll carry on for now. When you are in position and ready, you have the Meditation music on and you are either sitting down or lying down. Close your eyes, take a deep breath in through your nose, and exhale through your mouth slowly, with each breath you are going slowly into relaxation, you feel your body start to relax with each deep breath.

As you go deeper but not to sleep! bring your attention to the third eye, which is the spot between your eyebrows. Focus your attention there, while breathing deeply in through your nose and out through your mouth. Just let what comes up on the screen of your mind. This is not a guided Meditation just for relaxation.

Let the colours flow on the screen, if it is anything else that you don't like then just tell it to go away and it will. You may have images of loved ones or other things like meadows, the experience is completely to the individual unless you are doing a guided meditation just depends on what you hope to gain from the experience of meditation and what is your aim? for some it maybe just for relaxation.

Some want answers or guidance in their life which there are guided meditations on these, some use meditation to manifest.

When you are finished keeping your breathing slow and deep, bring your senses back around by thinking of sending signals to your body parts and move them slowly move your fingers and toes, when you are ready open your eyes.

Now how do you feel after doing some meditation? for me, I feel tons better. Now I can do this instantly like asking spirits to provide me with a car parking spot if I know where I am going will be packed. I have done it many a time and it worked.

I take deep breaths without closing my eyes and imagine a car parking space available to me and see it with my third eye (me driving into that car parking space), when I get to the car park in question, it may not be the same space I imagined but there will be a space available to me. It works every single time.

I imagine myself on that frequency I'll talk about frequencies in another chapter. Which is part of manifesting, again this is difficult to start with, but with practice, it is easy as pie.

The power within us is so great, it is mind-blowing. Just breathing deeply is relaxing. Have you ever had problems falling asleep because you have so many things going around in the mind and brain, which just won't shut up and give you a break to sleep even though you could sleep standing up?

I tried fantasising about the future which usually works, but occasionally it doesn't and hours have passed. What I do then is quite literally tell the brain and mind to shut the F up it is time for sleep. If that fails, I then tell myself whatever it is that I am concerned about that is stopping me from sleeping can hold off until morning as there is nothing I can do about it now and it is robbing me of my sleep and I deal with it in the daytime.

I meditate when I'm manifesting things, sometimes I can be just watching TV and just zone out on Autopilot and just think about all sorts of stuff and what is bugging me and life in general.

I use mediation when I am struggling to come up with something to talk about on my YouTube channel, It's my way of asking for help when I'm struggling, I may not get the answer straight away it may take a couple of hours, can even be days and weeks but I always get my answer.

I have been using mediation to get help from the universe in order to write this book. I have been known to autotype, I zone out while typing but my fingers keep typing away as I think about other stuff lol.

There is magic and power within us, I sometimes even surprise myself about how powerful I am, as in spiritually and how much I can do if I just put my mind to it. Take this book for example it has been tough going and has a big learning curve.

When I started writing this book I could only manage to write about 500 words a day, and then I pushed myself to write 1000 words, then 1,500 and now I pushing 3,000 words a day. I am improving all the time next step will be 5,000 now seems very daunting to me, just like 3,000 was last week. In order for me to get passed this, I meditate and ask for reassurance and I usually get a spiritual hug and kiss from my husband that is now a spirit.

I am doing a lot of instant meditation just lately sometimes just to get through the day that includes drinking a lot of tea as well. Which I needed yesterday after writing the 3,000 words the other day.

I really pushed myself to get to the 3,000 word goal I had hit the wall like people do in a marathon. At the moment it is in the middle of summer and it is really hot in the mid 30's now that is hot for the UK, Harvesting crops has stopped because of the heat as it is now a fire risk.

Sorry gone off of course there, it's a little break for me and I come back around to the subject in question, meditating! Some people use it to just get through the day like I did yesterday. It is a powerful tool within us, and guess what it's free to use so excuse of, oh I cannot afford to meditate.

The next excuse is not having the time to meditate, if you want it you'll find the time, even if it is instant meditation, that is still meditation. I'm sure you can find 5 minutes in the day for meditation.

Meditation can be from 5 minutes to 5 hours or longer like the Buddhist monks who can meditate for days without eating, drinking or going to the toilet!! How they do it I do not know, but they do. It is amazing what the mind and body can do when they are in complete harmony with each other.

I love doing meditation, maybe one day I'll learn to teach it and write a whole book on Meditation instead of just a 2,000 word piece chapter.

Meditation can be used to balance your chakras which may sound a little hippie and new age, the thing is Meditation has been going on since our existence. Back with the cavemen and women. Which only a select few kept the tradition and passed it on to others and it has sort of stuck to the hippies/gypsies/fortune tellers/native Americans/new age folk/Buddhist Monks and so on. I may of missed a few people off that list but you get the gist.

So meditation can be used for different things. This is how I understand Meditation and what I have picked up through my lifetime on this earth. As I try and use it everyday. As life can get stressful, I use instant meditation in order to push myself and hit my targets. I have targets in order to grow and expand my mind, and learn more.

Life can be challenging and by using meditation, it gives me the time I need to revaluate myself on where I am going and what is my next step in order to grow as I have mentioned before I even use it to relax and calm myself down when I feel that I am getting frustrated, stressed and finding it hard to cope a particular situation.

I will keep adding little stories of my experience and what I have learned within this book in order for you to understand it better and how they have helped me.

I love sharing this stuff, and helping others, I do not like seeing people suffering, as I too have suffered many things, I have empathy towards people that are suffering like I did, but cannot see the light at the end of the tunnel. It is frightening to say the least.

Meditation is starting to become a habit of mine that I use throughout the day. It's like going on a day trip to the magical realm where everything is possible.

9

Chapter 9 : Gratitude

Gratitude is another key to success. I do a gratitude log everyday, I say thank you to everything and everyone I meet.

In the morning when I wake up, I say "Thank you for another great day and let it be a pleasant day. May I have guidance today please, Thank you".

The gratitude log I do everyday is 10 things I am grateful for that day like, I am grateful for one) a microwave, two) my car, three) the roof over my head, four) my washing machine to wash my clothes, five) The shower so I can clean myself, six) my laptop so I write my books, Severn) Shampoo to wash my with, eight) soap for cleansing my body, nine) my dog for company, ten) the air that I breathe.

That gratitude log is not the same everyday. It is different everyday as there is so much to be grateful for. When I have reached one of my goals I am grateful that I have reached it and that I give myself a little treat as a celebratory win. It also depends on how big the goal was for me.

Right now I am grateful for a cup of tea which I am grateful for water, a kettle, electric, the plug socket from where the electricity is coming from and that has come down an electric cable and into my flat and into the kettle which then boils my water that has come out of my kitchen tap that has been sent through underground pipes after it has been cleaned so it is ok to drink, clean and wash up with.

Do you see where I am going with this? There is so much we take for granted that are perfectly normal everyday things, yet here they are in existence everyday. How many people and objects are involved in making one cup of tea?

One cup of tea is a simple little thing that we do not even think about, we don't even think of all the people and things that have had to come together just to make that cup of tea.

Life is so much better with gratitude, My life has turned around since having gratitude and saying thank you for absolutely everything. Life is better living with gratitude than being angry, mad, jealous, mean, worried, fearful, in pain and having miserable existence.

Having gratitude makes one feel good on the inside and it raises your vibration so the good stuff can come. Then gets passed on to the next person and then the next, it's very infectious but it's good and does the world good too.

Smile and the world smiles with you. Have gratitude and good things will come your way guaranteed. It's a natural law. People will be thankful for you instead of mean and nasty. I do hope this is making sense and is helping you.

I am doing my best to put it into simple terms as there is no need to overcomplicate things. When I first got into this I was confused and I thought I understood it until I started experimenting and looking back over my life and when I got what it is I wanted. How did that occur, and how I did make them happen? Was it magic?

I looked into the details of what I did before that event happened, and following Bob, listening to what he was saying it resonated within me was true. The more it resonated the more I followed Bob and the others that spoke about this subject.

I know I will live with gratitude until I pass on over the other side and continue with gratitude on that side too. My life has improved since having gratitude and it's part of me and there is no way will I go back to living without gratitude.

Living without gratitude made my life hard in getting what I want, I tried different marketing companies just to get by and make a little bit of money to make my life just that little easier. The only thing is I never sold anything until I started having gratitude for the little things like a cup of tea, Sleeping and the air I breathe.

I now choose to look on the positive side of life, doesn't matter what it is. Even the bad experiences have positive lessons. If you look for the positive you will get the positive, look for the negative and you'll get the negative. You get what you are looking for.

If you struggle to get ten things you are grateful for then just be grateful for at least one thing a day and I promise you it will get easier. The more you look the more will come.

I am grateful for all the spiritual guidance I am receiving to help get this book written and the encouragement to meet my writing goals. I am grateful for how far I have come over the past couple of days and how much work that has gone into this book and its chapters.

I really do hope it helps people, I am grateful that it is me writing it and how much I am learning as I write it. Plus how much it is helping me grow and get stronger.

I am falling in love with this book and writing it lol. This is my passion, I maybe finding it hard to write right now as it is so hot in the UK and I am dripping water everywhere, and finding it hard to concentrate as my glasses are getting steamed up and is difficult to see through them I will carry on and push through.

At least I am not here shivering in the cold, with cold fingers. I have made the decision to write x amount of words and I will keep to that promise, through sheer determination and will which I will come that in another chapter.

I am grateful for my sheer determination, will, faith and my stubbornness. If I say I am going to do something nine times out of ten I will carry out that said item.

It is a good thing to have all those that I have said, they make things happen. When I get an idea wild horses will not move me off the idea. The idea will be set in stone.

Having gratitude that I already have the possession of the thing that I want can bring that item to me even quicker. I love the saying 'Have the attitude for gratitude.'

It just puts everything into perspective, you'll see life in a whole new way. You'll never look back and return to the old ways of seeing things. You'll have a new attitude on life and good things will happen.

All you have to be is patient, be patient with yourself. Believe me, when you have gratitude for life and everything in life things will turn into good things. They may not happen straight away but your feelings can change straight away like night and day.

If you going to start anywhere, start with love in your heart and love will be returned to you. I suggest you re-read this book over and over again as you will not get it all the first time you read it, repetition is key to learning new stuff and be relaxed when you read it as you'll absorb more information when you are relaxed.

Be proud of all your little wins and BIG wins be proud of yourself if you don't no one else will lol. Life is for living. I am grateful that I can write and have a laptop to do it on. I am grateful I have money coming to me.

I do have posters to help everyday to encourage me to keep going when I am not feeling at my best. I have my little goals to keep me going otherwise I will procrastinate and watch TV all day.

I want to help others with this book of mine and could be the last one I write like this, as I want to write for children and write different stories. So writing this book is something big for me. Yes, I keep going off track to try and help you understand without making to complicated and hard to understand.

It is helping me to write better, and understand myself, and thus helping you. Have gratitude every single day and you will not regret it, you'll have a new lease on life. Having a bit of gratitude will change the day you experience.

I choose to have gratitude everyday and it has improved my life to no end. Everything I do I have gratitude for, even little simple things that we take for granted everyday.

Having gratitude changes things and the way you look at things, it helps overcome fear. amongst other things. It really does improve your quality of life, it has mine.

It helps me to carry on with whatever I am doing. At the moment as I write this the gratitude I have for all that I have written so far is encouraging me to carry on even though I want to just go and chill out somewhere and stop writing for the day.

Other than gratitude I have a deadline to get this finished so I can have some time off writing which is pushing me forward. I know I will be done for the day soon. I am grateful for my sheer determination to push me out of my comfort zone so I can grow and help others.

That was a little example of gratitude that I have. Yes, I put a fair few of those in this chapter as to give an idea of gratitude and what I am driving at. If you see the change within you then congratulations are on your way to living a full of life of happiness, joy, love and pleasantness.

It can be overwhelming at first but once you are over that, you will have a great life of happiness forever. Things will just fall into place like magic! You are allowing yourself to come into harmony with what you love, the better life will be.

I am well on my way to changing my mindset and my autopilot, it maybe putting up a fight but the mindset I want will win in the end. Everything is changing in my life for the better because of my attitude of gratitude.

I just want to keep going now, and do not want to stop for anything lol. I've even forgotten about my cup of tea I made myself and only drank half, at least I drank some of it before it went cold. Must have been what I needed to carry on working.

I am grateful for that cup of tea and now I am cooling down as the evening is drawing in. I am so happy at this point I could burst into tears but I will not. Life is great, my heart is full of gratitude and is it swelling up. I can feel it, it is even skipping a beat I am so full of Love, gratitude and happiness that it is overflowing into my work and I hope you feel it too.

I am at peace with this book as I write I feel that it will not need editing, as I am editing as I go which is different to what I have been told. I will of course edit it after I finished writing it.

Now I am thankful for editors as editing is a big job, writing is the easy part it is what comes next in order for it to be in print. Not only is editing a big part is an important part including proofreaders for which I am also grateful.

I will now move on to the next chapter: Faith. Should be a good chapter, looking forward to writing it.

10

Chapter 10 : Faith

Faith is the same as believing in the impossible. Without faith, you have fear and doubt and you are on the negative vibration more on this later.

Look at religion, for example, many religions pray to an unseen God or Goddess and those that do pray and to the onlooker seem to be talking to thin air. Those that are praying have the faith that their God or Goddess is listening to them and will answer their prayers in one-way shape, form or another and that to me is faith.

In order for anything you have asked for to materialise, you must have faith that it will appear in one-way shape, form or another and it may come from somewhere quite unexpected.

You must have an understanding as well. Faith is a positive emotion and a powerful tool. Faith is the ability to see something on the screen of your conscious mind that no-one else can see, to see the invisible and to believe in the incredible.

Faith is the power that permits you to receive what others call impossible. So have faith with an understanding of how the mind works. And you too can move mountains.

Having in your heart that what you want will come to pass and all your dreams will come true, if you have any doubt at all, that will hinder and make your dreams come to you slower. Have faith in yourself that you can bring your dreams into reality.

I have faith in myself to finish this book on time this time around. Why is that? I have faith to push myself just beyond my limits so I can grow and share this information with the world.

When I was learning to drive, I had the faith and determination to pass my driving test whatever it cost, I believed in myself like I did when I published my first book and I will continue to have faith in myself to have my dreams and reach my goals.

I pretty much have lots of doggie determination, I'm like a dog with a bone. I will not give up on anything that I want, even if I am in pain with my arthritis I will get it done.

If I promise something I will deliver, I have faith in my abilities. I have faith in myself that I will continue with my YouTube channel as I have turned it into a habit. I have faith money comes my way when I need it.

Faith is part of our emotions and it is an emotion. I have given a couple of examples just now to give an idea of faith if you never thought about faith or understand it.

I cannot see my husband but I can feel him close by, I can feel his energy I trust myself enough to know it is a fact, I cannot prove it scientifically but I have faith in myself to know he is there.

Having faith excludes all doubt. I may go off track here. Just hear me out. I repeat what I have said in order to help you and teach you something that may not of known, repetition is key to learning. We have knowledge but without action, it is just useless information.

So if you have been to college or university but haven't fulfilled that job you wanted, take a look at yourself and ask yourself why. Ask yourself why haven't gone after your dream job if you have the degree for it.

Are you doubting yourself as I did with my first book that is why it took so long to get it published, I doubted my skills as a writer, there are writer jobs out there for me but I have never taken a course in writing until quite recently who are teaching me.

Other people had faith in me that I could pull it off, but not me. Eventually, I plucked up the courage and got it published now I am living my dream as an author. Which is what I wanted to do since I was little.

I was hanging around with the wrong people that were putting me down and feeding me negative energy and saying to me that I would never be an author. That changed when I decided to change who I hung around with.

Instead of hanging people who were always talking negatively not just to me but in general. I started to hang around with positive people instead and follow Bob Proctor.

I'm not here to judge you. I suggest you start hanging around those that are positive and will courage you to after your dreams. I did and look at me now. I am not saying cut ties with old friends and family but just keep them at arm's length while you grow more positive and they will follow you eventually.

Have faith and never look back at what once was, the future is better and more positive. Live in the here and now not the past or future we only have the now. We can shape our futures now.

We do not know how much time we have left on this planet earth. Make it the best with what you have and be grateful for it everyday. I know am rambling on a bit, I just love writing what's on my mind and I get into the flow, and there are no brakes!!

I think like the mask here, "Somebody, stop me". I don't have pain in my wrist at the moment while I am typing away only when I stop typing. How powerful is the mind!!

Faith is removing doubt from your mind, it is a powerful tool for reaching your dreams and goals. Faith replaces self-doubt. We have to know what we want and have faith that we will receive it.

I'll talk about this later on, but I am going through the Laws and Principles including emotions not necessarily in order but the basics in achieving the change in autopilot that we desire, I will put it in the summary at the back of the book. I do not want you to jump to the back of the book now, you need to read the book and re-read it. It is meant for you to take in the information contained in this book. It is not to be devoured in one sitting.

I want to help you with this subject a bit like Bob Proctor. Changing our autopilot and mindset is no easy feat it does take time, so yes I may off track from time to time as I want this book to come off as friendly and chatty not as a guide.

I have faith in myself that I can pull this off, I may find it difficult at times but I am learning myself, I hope you are relating to what I am saying. The books I have read come off as guides not friendly and chatty like I would like them to be, so I am creating one, go me!!

Having faith is believing something is going to happen or believing miracles do happen to those who have faith in their God. Faith is the ability to see the invisible, to believe in the incredible and it is the power that permits you to receive what the world calls the impossible. There I am quoting Bob Proctor from his six-minutes to success programme.

It's helping me get back into the zone again. I feel like I have a mountain to climb here, I have faith I will get to the summit! I have given myself this big task because I have let myself down and my schedule slip so I am now pulling myself up by my bootstraps and cracking on with it.

Faith is a very powerful tool and emotion and you have it understand it for it to work. I no longer worry about as much stuff anymore as I have faith that whatever I ask for I shall have it.

When I wanted my dog, Edith, I visualised myself with her and taking her on walks by myself around my area where I lived even going on holiday with her and eventually she was mine, I didn't need money to make that decision. I had faith that she would be mine and be living with me no matter how she came to live with me.

I set out and brought all the stuff I needed to look after her, I brought her feeding bowls, toys, poo bags and a bed. I have never owned a dog before, I have only ever owned a cat, hamster, rabbit, rats and fish. I have looked after dogs and been trained in how to look after them but never owned one.

If she was to go, I would be lost without her. When I go on holiday without her I am at a lost end in the evenings and mornings especially as they are normally the times I take her for a walk and during the day when I am not writing.

So faith is important but you have to understand it, because one bump in the road can send you off course and lose all faith without an understanding. I know this may not make sense right now because I keep going off track with these little examples.

I know this book is on Manifesting but Manifesting goes in hand with changing our autopilot.

Do you want to change your life? if so read on and bear with me. once you understand all this then changing our autopilot will be as easy as pie, trust me.

I may ramble on because I want you to understand this, and everything will just slot into place just like a jigsaw, all the pieces are coming together to improve your life.

Faith is just one of the pieces to understand along with all the other pieces to help you change and you have to be willing to change for it all to happen. The will is the next chapter, but the chapters are not in the right order, I'm sure you can figure it out.

Life is worth living if you have the faith to change your autopilot, which is not taught in schools. Have faith in yourself to reach your goals they maybe big or small. Either way, they are your goals and no one else's.

Have the faith the carry out the necessary tasks to reach your goals and dreams. I have faith in you, go for it. Do not let anyone get in your way. Just breathe in that love, feels wonderful doesn't it?

Use your imagination to see what you desire, and feel as if it is already yours, you are living it. What a wonderful feeling, do this everyday. Positive energies will be coming your way on the wings of love.

I think I have covered the subject of faith quite a bit now. I love having faith it makes everything possible, and everything tastes so much sweeter. The dreams in the night are better. Everything is better with faith no matter what religion you belong to or whether you do not have a religion, it does not matter.

You do not have to belong to a religion in order to have faith, just have faith within yourself, and you will not regret it, I maybe a spiritualist and yes we do lose faith in ourselves sometimes but as long as you get back on the horse all is ok.

Love life, it is worth living. I am doing what I love doing.

11

Chapter 11 : The Will

Do you know the will is what gives your mind real power? You have power in your mind, you must have the will to access it.

You see the will, you learn to concentrate with it. The will to the mind would be like a magnifying glass with the sun. It marshals the energy and brings it in zeroing on one spot. Now I'm going to give an exercise on concentration. Take a pen, a chair and a blank wall. With the pen put a dot on the blank wall, and take a seat in your chair opposite the wall that you are facing and that you have just drawn a dot on.

Don't tell anyone you are doing this. No-one's going to see it. And if they do they will think it's a fly. Now, your five minute exercise is to concentrate on that dot. Bring your mind to focus on the dot. Until you mentally become one with the dot Now, if your mind wanders, bring it back to the dot. Don't feel bad that your mind wandered, just bring it back to the dot. Now, practice this everyday for the next 90 days.

You may say, my goodness, no. Do it. It'll take great dividends to concentrate on that little dot. When you learn to concentrate on one thing you can concentrate on anything.

The above statements and exercise have come from the great Bob Proctor himself and I am passing it on to you. There will be more from him as we go on.

Concentration increases the amplitude of vibrations. What does that mean? You're going to give real power to your thoughts.

You see, thought waves are cosmic waves. When you send out a wave of energy, even if it's just idle thinking there's not much power until you are concentrating on it, then it's more powerful.

All the pros in any field have the power of concentration. Concentration is one of the keys to success and it's done with the will. The dot. Focus on it.

A good chunk of that is from Bob Proctor I have changed the wording slightly to help you understand better.

There's is truth in the old saying "where there's a will, there's a way" and there is no truer word. The will to get through things that seem tough at the start and you look back and think that was easy what was I worried about, and that is part of overcoming your fears as talked about in a previous chapter.

I have the will to push through and past my comfort zone in order to keep writing even though my brain and body want me to stop and take a break, I will not let up until I have done what I set out to do. I am hot and exhausted if stop just for 5 minutes I will want to throw in the towel for today.

My will power is a lot stronger than that, so I will keep going. I have the will power and determination to finish what I started. Will power on its own is not enough the other pieces of the jigsaw have to come together as well.

Having will power you can push past your comfort zone and grow, I have mentioned this in the previous chapter that I have had the will power and determination to succeed in passing my driving test along with many other things I wanted in my life.

I know it is a very powerful force as it is attached to our emotions like many of the subjects in this book. A little bit like hulk but not in physical form. Add any emotion and the will is then super strong.

Some people call me stubborn, that I maybe but good stubborn. When I get an idea there's a really good chance I will see it through and no one will change my mind.

You have to have will power to make things work. Even though you may not have the money or know-how, which will come as you learn a skill and start putting it into practice.

If you have the will to succeed, you'll have the will to get the money for it. Make a quick and snap decision on something anything longer than 30 seconds is too long and you will not have the will to follow it through.

Making quick and snap decisions sets up the vibration that will flow from your mind and through your subconscious and move your body into action, but you also need an understanding for it. This includes having passion and desire for whatever it is that you want.

The will, will drive you to your destination, you bring the passion, the desire, and an understanding of the laws and principles of nature.

If you have a burning desire to change, you will change. If you want it then go for it no excuses, You will find the money needed to fulfill your desire. There is always enough money.

Be grateful for what your desire is already in your possession, no one can take it away from you unless you let them. No one can control you unless you let them but think about the consequences of your actions.

I know there is a lot of red tape about, but never mind that, if you have dreams of being a successful Author then go it, do not let anyone tell you any different, if you want to be a teacher, a celebrity, an actor, singer, a driver, shop keeper, a librarian, or even a gardener whatever it maybe go for it.

If it's your life's purpose do it with passion even if it's just to entertain people it doesn't matter unless it matters to you. You are in charge of your life and how you feel, I know I have gone way off track here. You can see what my passion is!!

I had the will to do what I want to do, not no-one else, some people want me to get a normal 9-5 job but that is not me, my passion lies here in these words. Helping people get what they want and need.

My next book after this one is going to be more entertainment value than this book which is educational value. I just want to get my point across and help people that are struggling with this concept just like I was.

I have heard people say life is what you make it and I've never understood that because I was looking from the outside in. Which is the wrong way round you must look from the inside out. Do not let the outside world control how you feel.

You are in control of how you feel no-one else, it's one error I have learnt. I have said this many times I am now choosing to respond not react to situations. Always love yourself first.

Everyone has will power to survive. If want it badly enough you will get it. This I learned by looking back over my life and seeing when I got something that I really wanted, with all of my heart, body and soul.

I had the passion and desire running through my body and it put my body into action. My will power drove me to my goals. That is how powerful the will is when added with passion and desire.

I never gave up smoking properly until I had the will power to quit for good. Understanding the will and how to kick it into action. Has changed my life, the will can even change your habits like I have just mentioned.

Never underestimate the will. It has the power to get you where want to go and bring your dreams closer to you, and drive you towards them, it has done it for me, it can do it for you as well.

Believe it, believe in yourself, and get that courage, the drive, passion and desire in your heart, body and soul. Life can be so different to the one you are living.

I'm on a new day of writing and everything told me not to do any writing today I was making excuses of why not to do it and put it off until another day, that is what I used to do and why I kept pushing the deadline back but now I have seen the error of my ways. I have learned about them yet again.

I have mentioned on my YouTube channel the date's that I will get this done by and the release date which looking back is a mistake, as I don't know when the release date is I am only guessing and making it up. I will know the release date once everything else is done and finished.

I have the will to get this in gear and get a move on now as I see the time is dwindling, I am running out of time to complete my task as I am getting on with it.

Only the will and determination are pushing me to finish this book on time. Otherwise, I'd be watching TV all the time but that does not help anyone and it doesn't help me finish this book.

It is still hot mainly in my little flat, it seems downstairs has the heating on!! outside it's nice and cool but inside the flat feels like a sauna it's nearly 7 degrees difference. So writing at the moment is taking a lot of will power to get through.

I am grateful for cups of tea and glasses of water to keep me hydrated. It could just be my will power alone pushing me to keep writing, and always remember to keep positive.

I am always grateful for my will power and which helped me quit smoking finally and with the help of the NHS and a couple of good friends.

The will can help you come through the most difficult of situations and quit when you need to quit something like a bad habit.

Remember to always ask yourself why are doing something when comes to changing a habit. Ask yourself "why am I changing this habit?" "Why am I doing this task what is the outcome of it?" "Who is it benefiting?" "Is there room for improvement?"

This is a way of getting the will into gear. That's what I did today, what would happen if I did not do any writing today, the answer was that I would keep doing it and the habit of that would form and this book would never get written or finished and another year would pass before it was finished.

I would of quite happily taken a nap but because the will inside of me said no the book needs finishing and the more words written today means less to do the next time and it will be out in time and helping others, especially if want to change lives today not next year or the year after.

The more I do the quicker it will get done and help someone, so no more excuses. Help will always be around to those who ask for it. There is someone out there in need of this book.

I use my will power to manifest what I want, with the will on my side I can keep focused on what I want to do I have just given an example of this. I maybe just be slightly distracted as we have a thunderstorm now and that I of which have been manifesting to cool the air temp down so I can sleep at night.

The air really needs freshening up around here. There are several steps to take to manifesting what you want I will go through these at the end of the book. I want you to read the whole book first.

12

Chapter 12 : Memory

Did you know that we all have a perfect memory? In order to realise that we have a perfect memory, we must exercise the memory cells in our brain.

There are ways to improve our memories. Like visual aids on the screen of our minds. Like picking up a duvet from the cleaners, on the screen in your mind put your duvet on top of the car then that should remind you to pick up your duvet from the cleaners on the way home from work.

Memory will develop through ridiculous association. One book Bob Proctor suggests getting is 'the memory book by Harry Lorraine and Jerry Lucas' available on Amazon.

Even your muscles in your body have memories so they can store the energy required for daily activities and you'll only burn off extra energy by changing your daily routine or a dance routine on a regular basis then your muscles will not only be stronger but also won't store the energy. It will use it up instead to make the muscle stronger.

I too am training my memory to improve, through ridiculous association and repetition. It works!! Sometimes I make a little chant up in order to remember things.

Sometimes we need to relax in order for memories to come back, think back to the time when you see a familiar face on a TV show and cannot think of their real name or what else they have been in and all of sudden when you are relaxing the name just pops into your head but you could not remember at the time of their name or what they appeared in.

The memory muscles can only get stronger if you work them more and focus on making them stronger if that is what you want, I have learnt as well from watching Sandy Gallagher and Bob Proctor on YouTube, that we have memories from the future which most of you will seem a bit far fetched.

I can promise you it is not. We have all heard people that literally dream about the future and then it comes into reality. Like someone dying in a certain way and they dream exactly that person dying the same way, they die without having any involvement with that person apart from being friends.

The friend could have had a dream of his friend dying in a car crash and then 5 days later their friend died in a car crash who is living about 500 or more miles away in exactly the same way they did in the dream a bit like a premonition, but this is a memory from the future for some reason could be to help us cope with what is to come and prepare us for it.

I too have had dreams like this, there is one dream I have had that is to pass still but it is in the pipeline of being built. I now meditate on that dream and ask for assistance in order for it to come into reality and let me tell you this it is some big. It is very very big but I am playing those cards close to my chest until it is time for it to be revealed. Only a handful of people know about it.

I am not ready for it to be known just yet, I am using meditation to use my future memories in order to build this said BIG item!! They are going to be helping me figuring what, how and when. Gotta love meditation and future memories to start growing something now.

This is part of having perfect memories, our future memories, they can help us in the here and now moment. A bit like this book, everything I talk about in here is part of manifesting, and bettering ourselves and life in general.

Mostly I think life is about figuring stuff out to improve not only our lives but the lives of others, take the motor car for example it wasn't invented by one person for himself, but to make other lives better and easier to get from A to B and much quicker than by foot alone.

By having a perfect memory we can remember what went wrong in the first, second, third or more goes until we get things into the right order and invent stuff like a mobile phone, a computer and even electricity. Everything may have been in existence in the ethos, we just needed to put things in the right order for them to exist on our plane of existence.

Did you know that you can change the way you feel from hot and sweaty to nice and cool just by the power of your mind, this takes a bit of practice. What I do is that I tell myself that I am nice and cool, I then keep saying it and soon enough I am nice and cool not hot and sweaty. Anything is possible with the power of the mind.

Gotta love all the manifesting material I'm putting here. I am in love with it. I'm addicted and I'm the one writing it!! all that I have learned from those that have gone before me is going into this book.

I can see changes in me that other people thought would never happen, I think differently from what I used to, and I act differently as well and that of the other week, changes can happen very quickly without you even noticing.

I believe in myself more, I trust myself more and I love myself more. I still get slightly distracted a little by the shinys but now I know what I want and I am going for it and I know my passions and what I love and like including my dislikes I know my heart and soul and what I want to do with my life.

I am not talking about the material world, what I would love to have. I'm talking about what I love doing and the why I love doing it. Money is just an energy now to me that is transferred for services rendered.

Money has not always been around, people used to trade services and goods to pay for services or goods. Read upon history way before the 1700s for that information some of that information may blow your mind clean away!!.

We have memories of the past, future and present right inside our minds and sometimes to gain access we have to meditate on them and ask ourselves to give access. We sometimes lock memories away because they are too painful and we do not want to know about them and we leave them locked away forever.

I know I'm off subject here and there, but it helps with keeping the flow nice and simple and chatty that is the reason for the short paragraphs so it's nice and easy to digest. If you need to stop anywhere you can and remember where you left off.

As I have said previously I want to keep this simple to understand by being light-hearted and chatty not like a how to guide. That is not me I want to do it gently and caring, unlike the other books I have read on this subject which can and I know make it all too complicated.

Those books were written by men and you can tell they were. Just by the way they write and the language men use. It's the way men are and how their brains are wired which are different to us females, that maybe the case but having a perfect memory is for everyone and everyone has a perfect memory.

That does not matter how we were wired, we all have perfect memories, absolutely everyone and I mean it, does not matter your background, colour, race, religion or sexual orientation. It does not matter who you are, you do have a perfect memory.

Make a habit of excising your memory daily and sure enough, it will improve. Without a doubt, it could even surprise you at how well you remember stuff. We make memories every single day of our lives but unless it is sufficient enough we do not remember but can we remember the day the answer is yes.

We just store that information in the do not need to know pile!! now, your thinking how on earth can we store all this information in our brain? We have part of the brain that controls memory we all know this and is just part of the brain that controls memory it does not store memory, a memory if I'm not mistaken, is part of the mind which is not a body part.

The brain is just like a switchboard, it does not hold memories. The brain controls how we remember and when we remember things. A bit like old age the brain cells decrease so we are told, so the ability to remember certain things naturally decreases and memories disappear that's not true, memories are still there but the access panel to them is no longer there or has some dodgy wiring going on!!

So memories can be a bit fuzzy lol. Especially those who get Alzheimer's they still have all the memories from childhood but not of yesterday. So the wiring is going a bit dodgy, so sorry to sound so crude, but it's the best way I can describe it at the moment.

Some people call it losing the plot on life, they are still a person who has lived for sometime and had way too much stress put on them which goes with nearly everything in this lifetime. When you have a rusted old shed that is falling to pieces, think about what that shed has been through before going out buying a new one that hasn't seen the light of day or has been rained on, the wind whipped around it trying to blow it over, been in freezing temperatures been snowed on.

All that stress of surviving will take its toll on anything that includes our bodies, the less stress you have the better. You are only as young as you feel that is another true saying. If you feel old and decrepit, you are going to be old, decrepit and grumpy! If you feel young, healthy and full of life then you will be young, healthy and full of life because that is what you expect to be and of course, you accept that is the way of life.

It does not have to be that way, take Bob Proctor for example he was fit and healthy until the last two weeks of his life and lived until he was 87, he was still running around making videos and talking to people as if he was still in his twenties. I do not know what happened in the last weeks of Bob's life but my thoughts and prayers go out to his family, he was a legend. He changed my life.

Bob's recordings will live on and change many more lives. I'll never forget Bob like my husband I will never forget him and he will never leave me.

So there you have it a perfect memory in a nutshell with added bonus material to boot. You might be feeling a bit worse for wear at the moment after that revelation, and in shock so grab yourself a brew or maybe a stiff drink more stuff to come!!

The next chapter is reason, and we all have a reason for doing stuff. There is reasoning behind everything, we may not understand it but it is there. I'll leave it there as this chapter is about memory and I touched upon some reasons why we have a poor memory.

I can not believe I did believe them. I know differently now, I know I have a perfect memory that needs to be trained from poor to perfect memory.

13

Chapter 13 : Reason

Reason, it's one of the most higher facilities and tools we have.

Did you know, that the late Dr. Ken McFarland said, 2% of the people think, 3% of the people think they think, and 95% of the people would rather die than think.

Now you are probably thinking everyone thinks. But no hardly anyone thinks at all. Mental activity is not thinking that's autopilot.

The reasoning factor gives us the ability in our conscious mind to take the power that is flowing through us. It flows into our consciousness and produces thoughts in our mind.

When you add one thought to another, you are building ideas. Through the power of reasoning, you can take and mould your thoughts and ideas.

Any idea can change your life for the better. For the next five minutes really think of what you could do better at, whatever it is you are doing. Five Minutes of concentrated thinking.

Remember mental activity is not thinking. Mental activity makes you a plaything for the outside world.

Begin to think, Really think. What are you going to do today? Are you going to improve your life for the better? How are you going to improve your life?

We give people reasons why we are doing what we are doing and reasons for not doing things that we said we would, you can blame the whole world for x, y, or z but you have the ultimate choice of how you feel and react to things and do them on autopilot.

We use reasoning everyday of our lives and do not know about it, as I just mentioned above only 2% think, 3% think they think and 95% do not even think. I know some days people that think they think and when they do think they are using energy up that is usually used elsewhere in the body. So they tire quickly by actually thinking.

I put my hands up to this I have done it, I am moving from the 3% club to the 2% club. Thinking for me is getting easier as I build my dream life. Building my dream life is not going to be easy and an overnight thing it is going to take time, patience, sweat, tears, blood, stress and a whole lot of joy, happiness and fun. Once I have built it, it will be helping others build their dreams it is so going worth the hard slog.

Improving people's lives for the better is my dream, Feelings that come when I improve someone's life for the better, my God I am on cloud nine. How am I going to feel in the future when I do this every single day.

Can you imagine your life improving for the better just by learning this material? There were times today that I wanted to put off writing today, I was trying to come up with excuses which are my reasoning for not doing it. The reason I started writing this book and my deadline were stronger than any excuse I could make up for not writing today. I have a weekend off after all.

Just one day of writing in pain, 3 hours of writing for one day and a weekend off, I know I won't get any done over the weekend because I have a friend over my number one fan. The reason is she will be talking to me all day long I will not get a word in edgeways so I will not be able to concentrate on what I am writing.

So there I was reasoning with myself, and pushing myself out of my comfort zone in order to help you and with my deadline looming I have to get on. It's like having an angel and a devil on each shoulder arguing about what is best.

I am giving you a clear example of reasoning not thinking. I am still adding bits from Bob Proctor and how he puts things, if I can understand it so can you. I have dyslexia and only just understanding this and writing it out is how I understand it, so you can too.

I have given myself a challenge to write so many words a day in order to get this book done on time and I am including my thoughts on how I am coping and learning this material. Including learning about the paradigms that are stopping me from doing what I want to do.

I know I keep going off track but that is how my brain operates, there are people out there whose brains operate similar to mine and never really understood this before, probably because when reading the other guides of self-help books they can come off a bit cold, odd and so the barriers come up and they never read another word in that book.

Then people go back down that downward spiral, and never making anything stick then they say that this stuff never works why? because they not thinking and do not understand it. I have taken the time to understand it and to help you to understand this in a light-hearted chatty way so people do not put the barriers up and give up.

That is a way that some people learn, in a heart-hearted chatty way so it is friendlier so all the reasoning and mental blockages can go flying out of the window!!

Please be aware reasoning is not bad or good, it is just a tool we use daily we make for whatever comes along we can use it to make excuses for not doing things or we could use it as a reason for doing something.

One lesson I have to share with you is when my husband passed at the early age of 42. This lesson I learned is that life is precious, short and worth living as if it was your last as we do not know when our last day is or how we going to pass on over to the other side into the spiritual world so be grateful for what you do have.

Reasoning is part of life and we can not live without it is part of us. It's part of our autopilot. With the reasoning tool, we have to make a reason why we do something good either in our life or someone else's.

We have reasoning on autopilot it makes excuses for us, yes you can change your autopilot but you must know and understand what you have on autopilot before you can change it.

If at any point I have any self-doubt about this book I tell it to do one, I tell it to P off, it's not welcome here. It's part of my paradigm trying to stop me with this book. It's my goal and dream to get this information out there and set it differently from the others.

Reasoning can happen quickly or take its time, we use reasoning when making decisions. I have heard people say all reasoning goes out of the window when family is involved but that is not true in my book. Reasoning is always there for every single decision we make whether quick or slow. It is always there playing its part in our life.

I suggest you stop and think about anytime when you have made a snap decision and why you made that decision. Now think of the time when you took your time in coming to a decision and why did you take your time in coming to that decision. I'll talk a lot more on decision later in another chapter.

Why did I carry on with wedding plans and marry the man of my dreams even though he was knocking on death's door, one) I thought he had a few years left in him, two) I loved him, three) I wanted to make his dreams come true before he passed, four) I was supporting him I was keeping his dreams alive.

Another example of reasoning there, I did not have to think of all those reasons when I kept up with the wedding plans my reason was out of love, I did it because I loved him and still do, and I will forever. I will never ever regret that decision yes it was painful when he sadly moved on to the other world.

I know that he is happy and healthy now, pain-free. We had our own reasons why we wanted to Italy for our honeymoon, but there were reasons why that was cancelled. Reasons are everywhere and we cannot get away from them.

We all have reasons for doing stuff or not talking to certain people. I know how this sounds but it is important that you understand it in order to change our autopilot.

Just like all the subjects I cover in this book they are all important in order to change our autopilot, Manifest what it is we want and we must understand them, I know I am sounding like a teacher saying this stuff lol.

I am learning everyday, everyday is a school day. I love learning and when I stop learning I am dead!! That's one major reason why to keep learning to keep living lol.

When we were young teachers made learning fun at school as that is how we learnt social skills and what have you. That is aim of nursery school and primary school to teach us, everyday key skills.

Where does this reasoning factor come from? I say it is inbuilt from where we were taught including our family and friends, and our influencers growing up, each of which makes up our teachings and our paradigms and habits. I think some of it is built into our DNA.

A bit like how we look and act, some come from around us, who we hang around with which is more important as we get older. Who we hang around with influences us.

We can change that like night and day just like Bob says. He has recalled a story of his many times, " I was in a pub in London drinking a pint of bitter, when I looked around and seen that everyone in here is bum! as they are always in here, so that must make me a bum too because I am always in here too like them. So I put my glass down and walked out. I have never been back there since and I never acted like that since that day and I never touched another pint of alcohol either."

Just like that, he changed a paradigm/a habit because he realised what he had become and he didn't like it so he changed it and of course, his reasoning came into play as well.

As you can see you might not even realise that your reasoning plays a big part in your life, no matter what we do or say, there is always a reason, and yes Bob had his reason why he shared that story over and over again at every seminar he ever did, every training he taught, even on the teachings on the YouTube videos he did. Including the free teachings.

Teaching us everything is possible, you just have to make your mind up and make committed decisions and stick to them, like I have done with this book, I made a promise to you and me that this book would be complete in a certain time frame and I am sticking to it even though my habits my paradigms are trying to stop me. I will not let them beat me lol.

Bob will always teach me from beyond the grave lol, I will keep his lessons close to me, close to my heart as his teachings have changed me, and those of my colleagues in Spear Business Solutions.

Grief has taught me a lot too, it has taught me to be thankful in my everyday life even if I am in pain, I am alive and it is a blessing.

14

Chapter 14 : Perception

Perception is a mental faculty. It's one of our higher facilities. It's one of those that separates us from the animal kingdom. Basically, it's different points of view.

On a piece of cardboard, there is a picture of a vase. One person looks at it and sees the vase another person looks at it and sees two faces. Some might say it's a difference of option. But it's different perceptions, One person sees one thing and someone else sees something else.

Perception is easy to get and I do not think it takes much understanding or explaining. People just look at the world differently some prefer and look for the negative things and see everything that is wrong. Some people like to look at the positive side of life and see everything that is right in the world.

On the exercise I just mentioned above comes from Bob Proctor, neither of the people are wrong, they just see things differently, where both are right it's a bit like the inkblot test in a doctor's office.

Here is an example, A clean and very tidy house can be that someone is either a germaphobe, they do not have anything else to do, they have cleaners in or it is not lived in so it's clean and tidy. Then you have the messy/cluttered house this house is definitely lived in they either do not have the money for cleaner, and prefer the house to look like it is lived in, or they do not have the time for housework because they are busy with other things, they could be busy making memories.

I know that was a poor example, but it still shows the difference in seeing things. In a nutshell, perception is basically seeing things in a different light, at a different angle

Seeing things from someone else's point of view, is in my eyes and the way I understand it. Seeing things from a different perceptive. There is no wrong or right answer, it just is neither or.

When you are just set in your ways, you can not see the other person's point of view or where they are coming from as it's your way or highway or no way, to be successful and build relationships you have to be respectful of each others opinion and point of view and come to a mutual agreement.

If you are struggling to come to terms with a business agreement with your business partner then best to take a step back and have a breather if you can re-arrange the meeting for another day that way you both get to think things through.

It is nice to have a break for a bit even just to mull things over, but not to overthink things as fear and doubt will take hold. I know this only too well, and then panic starts flowing as well which then leads to stress and all those negative emotions. Then you are on that downward spiral into hell!! Lol.

I love writing but it is also nice just to step away when I get a mental block and think about what else put, or how I am to explain that. If I need assistance I either call on a friend, mediate it or go for a walk with my dog.

Understanding perception is an important key to being successful in all of your dreams, along with the rest of the keys in this book. It is as important as breathing and your heart pumping. As I may have mentioned all the keys need to be in order for it to work.

Having all the keys in the right order is a must. You must also have a passion for it, a burning desire for it. Have clarity of what you want this I will get back to it later.

It is just little something to keep you going. A little gentle reminder if you will. Remember one really important key is change, change your paradigms, your habits and your autopilot. Doing things naturally without thinking.

Thinking with a different mindset will allow your perception to change of other people, they have a life too but they see things differently to you. Be ok with that, people may like different things to you.

If we all had the same taste, looks, style, and lifestyle life would be really boring!! Think positively and it flows right to you, look on the positive side of life, and have fun. Everything is not all doom and gloom, it can be merry and bright, and lots of fun. Without downs, we wouldn't know what the ups were.

Take moving for example it can be really stressful for everyone involved including pets, but once you have settled into your new home you are happy and peaceful and get to enjoy life once again like Christmas with all the stress in the build-up and on the day everyone is having fun and getting along or they should get along. Same for wedding planning and everything should really be happy at the end of the day.

We get upset and angry when something does not work or has broken down and when they are fixed or we get a new one we are happy and overjoyed that something works. We are happy when something is going right.

We also take things for granted thinking they will always be there, so remember gratitude and what I said about it.

What have I covered so far: Gratitude, faith, the will, reason, memory, meditation, love, The mind, Happiness, Overcoming fear, seeing is not believing, and our conditioning.

I am still to cover: Imagination, Decision, The law of vibration and The law of attraction. So still a bit to cover and I have covered a lot. I really do hope you are getting value out of this and enjoying it as well.

I have spoken a bit on perception and how it is just seeing things in a new light or at a different angle and you see something new or something completely different.

Changing our mindset, changes our attitude and the way we act. Which is moving us in the direction we want to go which is up because who wants to move down. Life is for expression and expansion.

Some people prefer just to drift through life and moan about life, Then you have those who want to make a life for themselves and their families, and there are those who just will try anything to get rich quick and rip off nice old ladies, they would even rip off their own nan just to get rich quick and they could not care for anyone. That is no life and not the way to go through life.

I know I'm off track here but go for your dreams, and live your dream life. People moan that they are not living their dream life and continue with the 9 to 5 life working for someone else when they can do whatever they love doing whether it be crafting, knitting, driving, fishing or cooking could even be in the media, a news anchor or scientist. Whatever it maybe go for it.

People love different things, I like knitting and crouching I even like driving but they are not my passions, my passions are helping people and writing so that is what I am doing, I am writing to help others live better lives. Am I filling someone else's pocket? no, I am not trading my time for money that is what a 9 to 5 job is.

Job in my eyes stands for Just Over Broke. I am going for my dreams and passions and no one is going to tell me otherwise. Feel worthy of your dreams, you can do it. Someone else may point out that a job is just a means to an end and security then you'll have someone point out that a 9 to 5 job is guaranteed money to live a good life.

There are many perceptions of the 9 to 5 job but neither is right or wrong it just is the way we look at it. Some people love doing 9 to 5 and you have others that don't. You have people that enjoy working from home for themselves, some people love working on farms, and others don't. Do you know what that is perfectly ok.

Getting perception and being ok with it, being ok that people have different thoughts and opinions is great that is what makes life great, I did ask for people's opinions on different covers for this book not long ago the results were interesting.

Just talking to different people and being open-minded to their views and how they see things really opens up your eyes to a whole new world and understanding.

It's interesting the different likes and dislikes of people and the different cultures and their backgrounds, how they have been brought up. Life is interesting.

I'm looking at myself now to what I was like 3 weeks ago, 3 months ago and years ago and what I have gone through to get where I am now, I see a difference from before I was married and just after I was married. I am totally different person.

People can change, they can change their mindset and even their whole body it's just like magic, nature is beautiful and amazing all at the same time, and we have more power than we realise. We can change ourselves it is possible.

We can change our mindsets, habits, the way we think, the way we act and our bodies. We can change it all, including the way we expect people to react to us.

Just change your perception of others and they can change the way they react to you. Every key and principle to change oneself for the better you have to love and respect them.

I know I am not going to win the hearts of everyone, because people have different perceptions of me. For me, people can either love me or hate me, but this matters to me of what I put out into the world, and what I write about I am passionate about.

I hope it helps people it does matter what your thoughts on me are, what matters is that you learn something and you take something from this book, I love helping people and writing.

People have different ways of doing things and you have different techniques in learning and teaching the same material as people see things differently to each other.

I prefer to teach through stories instead of being firm and authoritative. I prefer the gentle touch that way the barriers, fears and anxiety does not get in the way of teaching. As I know as I do when you come across as authoritative some people throw up barriers and then they cannot learn because the barriers are stopping them from learning.

I too have done that until I learned to lower those barriers as I wanted to know and learn about this subject I learned to understand my fears and why I wasn't learning and understand it, and a good chunk of it was that I wasn't ready I thought I was and I did not know that I was throwing up the barriers to the nicest of people and judging them negatively towards them.

Until I understood why and I took a step back to understand myself in the first place when all the other people were doing was trying to teach me in an authoritative way.

I was angry at them and sending out negative and horrible thoughts to them for being them. As I stood back and realised what I was doing that my thoughts and feelings began to change as I shifted my perception of people.

Sometimes we need to take a step back and take in the whole world not just our little world that we live in.

15

Chapter 15 : Imagination

Imagination what is it? Are we allowed an imagination as adults? Or is imagination just for kids? The short answer is yes, as adults we are allowed an imagination.

Imagination is where it all starts. Everything you see around you was first created in the imagination of someone. It's part of the world of vibration, it starts the imagination and then goes on to the conscious mind which in turn presses into the subconscious then the vibration travels through the body and into results.

Using the imagination to manifest is the foundation of manifestation. In the words of Bob Proctor "if you can see it in your mind then you will be able to see it in the physical world. We live in an ocean of motion, nothing is ever still everything vibrates."

I used my imagination to get my little dog Edith, I fantasised about Edith before I got her, I imagined Edith in my life and added all emotions of Edith being mine and along with playing, feeding, walking her and taking her everywhere with me.

When I wanted to learn to drive and everyone told me I wouldn't be able to drive for one reason or another. I imagined myself driving and passing my test, which came true after a while as I was determined to prove everyone wrong.

I use my imagination to manifest what I want and I meditate on them, from meditating I go into my imagination and start fantasising about what I want. I will repeat this process daily until I get it.

Allow yourself to use your imagination it does not matter how old or young you are. You have access to the most powerful tool you have to hand and guess what it's free to use for how long you want and you don't have to return it to anyone it's all yours for free!! How amazing is that?

That is fantastic all creators like authors, actors, directors, writers and inventors use it everyday. Imagination is great even when you are stressed you can relax and go into a meditative state and go into your imagination where anything is possible.

I love using my imagination and adding all the emotions I have at the touch of my hand, it helps me manifest what I want and I fantasise about what I want and where I want to go and with who I want to go with, including what is happening and other peoples responses. I fill my heart with love, joy, happiness and gratitude when I do this. It motivates me into action in order to manifest what I want, all I have to do is decide what I want.

I'll talk about decisions, and what is it that you want in another chapter along with the law of vibration and the law of attraction in the following chapters and getting confidence.

You use your imagination to send signals and messages to the universe and to your body, use your imagination to believe in yourself, gain love, hugs, kisses and motivation etc.

You use your imagination to receive as well not just to send out. Use your imagination to visualise what you want.

Imagination is always there and always working whether we know it or not, take for example that you have rang a certain person for a number of times and you expect them to either ring you back, turn up on the doorstep or answer the phone after you have tried contacting them for a number times and it's out of their character not to answer you, so your imagination goes to work, you start to imagine all sorts of horrible stuff that has gone wrong.

Yes, you are imagining it and it can come true whatever you are imagining. It is frightening it plays on your imagination and it goes into our dreams to figure this information out and it can make imagination work and winds us up. Until the situation has been resolved.

You can put a stop to that and use your imagination for good and imagine everything is good and ok to keep ourselves calm and not get worked up. Only imagine good things are happening instead of the worst things.

Artists and painters use their imagination to create pieces of art, that includes photographers, earning them some quite substantial amounts of money. They see what they want to create by putting the image on their minds' eye and start by putting pencil to paper.

Business people and entrepreneurs do the same when building a business from scratch they see the end product and where they want to be and with their imagination, they work backwards to where they are, then they move forwards with each planned step which was planned using their imagination.

I can only imagine what my life is going to be like next year and how it is going to be different from this year. I use my imagination to visualise this as I only have one book out at the moment and I plan to write many more after writing this book and publishing it, which are already in the pipeline and I am working on them as well.

I love doing this, as I use my imagination to visualise my future with at least 3 books published and working on many more and living in my dream home in Cornwall. I know this will come true for me as I am working on reaching my goals as write my books.

I can feel them happening. I use my emotions when I use my imagination and fantasise which is ok to do as it brings your dreams into reality, our manifesting powers are attached to our emotions, and emotions have power.

Emotions are power, and they are powerful. So use them with your imagination and you can manifest with your emotions and imagination which in turn puts you in the vibration of what you want and puts you into action.

That action brings you what you want, have the love and gratitude for it. Have the gratitude that it is already yours use your imagination as if you already have what you want how does that feel?

Anything is possible with your imagination, you can be as fit and healthy as an ox you just have to approve it and accept it as the truth. Things can be put on the screen of your mind and then reflected into what you are seeing like magic.

Feelings and emotions are powerful. I did this when I had a desire for a child even though I did not realise what I was doing at the time but looking back now I can see what I was doing and how I did it.

Not just having unprotected sex, I manifested it as I thought no matter how many times we did it, I wouldn't catch and I would be unable to have a child no matter how much I desired it. I used my imagination teamed with my feelings and emotions for it.

I put myself in that vibration of pregnancy and childbirth, holding my baby girl in my arms which then came true for me. I used meditation to put myself in that vibration and to see myself pregnant and going through the emotions of it all.

We all have this ability, we have the ability to change our lives for the better. It is within us to do so. If we want it badly enough it will come to us. We can put ourselves on that vibration through imagination, emotions, feelings, meditation and the will with memory and reason. Understanding all of this what I have put together including the laws and principles and what I have missed out so far.

Imagination is one of the key elements required for improving our lives and getting, and doing what we want. Without it, we will fail. They all need to be put in the right order.

Use imagination for good and contact the world through any means possible. Use imagination in your meditation.

Life is so much better with imagination, using your imagination to act the way expect to act when you have reached your dreams, by using your imagination this way you are changing your autopilot.

I do this everyday as I used to play games all day everyday. Now I still play games but not as much as it is not on my autopilot anymore writing is on autopilot and making YouTube videos is now on my autopilot.

I have turned my passion into a habit and that habit can and will turn into money as I am moving up to that frequency where I want to be. I am putting myself there through my imagination and using the power of my emotions and feelings in order to get there and help you do the same.

A little experiment for you, relax yourself in a comfortable position sitting down or lying down the choice is yours. You can go into meditation here if you so wish.

Think of what you really want and how you want to act. Now imagine yourself in that place, surrounded by the things you want. put yourself in that position in your imagination add emotions feel the love and joy of being there in that situation how do you feel? Your eyes can be open or closed.

If you want a more powerful feeling do this in front of the bathroom mirror and look closely into your eyes focus on your pupils let them glaze over as you enter your imagination let it flow, and allow yourself to feel those emotions of reaching your goals and dreams.

You can now feel those emotions even more powerful as you are looking inside yourself into your soul which is amplifying your feelings and emotions. If cannot feel anything then it's time to ask yourself why have you blocked your imagination, feelings and emotions.

It's time to block them, and allow yourself to feel all emotions across the range, happy and sad emotions. Without the bad, we cannot have happiness. If you have a teary moment that's ok as you are letting go of that emotion and feelings.

Letting go means that you allowing new and good stuff into your life, and letting go of the old and that which has no use to us. If you are feeling great then you are well on the road to your dreams and changing your autopilot.

Use your imagination to help you achieve what you want to achieve. With what I put in this book should help you achieve your goals and dreams. I love my imagination I use it daily every morning and night and use it for hours on end imagining my future and what it will be like when I reach my dreams and goals.

I have to get into the habit of imagining that I have them now in my present moment otherwise they will always be in the future and I will never have them, so watch this space in how I am doing this, bringing my dreams and goals to me.

If I can do it so can you. Get out there live the life you want, and become the expert in your field and get paid for doing so. Don't ever think you cannot do it because you can, you have the power to do so.

Imagination allows you to do anything, and live the way you want to live. I am doing what I love doing, which is helping others live better and to entertain others which is the pipeline that includes teaching what I am passionate about.

I love this world with the help of my imagination I can live and do what I want adding a sprinkle of joy, happiness, love and gratitude into the world. That then spreads to each other.

I can use my imagination to be pain-free and breathe easy, live by the sea enjoying my life writing books. Life is good and worth living with so much good in life, I am at peace with myself.

16

Chapter 16 : The Law of Vibration

We live in an ocean of motion, nothing is ever still, everything moves. I love that saying. We live in an Ocean of motion. Nothing rests.

You know the body in the coffin, we say it's dead but it is not. It still moves but to the naked eye, it is still. well, If nothing is created or destroyed, that would only postulate the theory of life. The body is not dead, the soul has moved out of it. The body still moving which you be able to see under a microscope. Get this if the body wasn't moving how would it ever turn to dust?! that's a heavy one to digest and take in!!

You know we are vibrating all of the time. Our brains are merely electric switching stations. Most people think their brain is their mind. Your fingernails and brain are part of your body. Mind is movement. When we think, we activate our brain cells, as we activate our brains cells we set up our body in a vibration

Your body is a manifestation of the movement from your mind. The vibration you are in is going to dictate how your body is going to move. Also dictates what is attracted to you.

I have heard Bob Proctor Talk about goals and he said "As you start to move towards the goal, the goal will start to move towards you."

Now the only things that you can attract to you are the things that are on the same vibrating field as you are. If you are worried and have doubts you are going to attract the things you don't want. But if you have a positive, powerful image on your mind you are going to attract a lot of stuff you do want.

It is a wonderful law to understand, In the secret, they talk about want, want turning into desire and desire sets up the vibration and vibration sets up the attraction.

You are pulling yourself to whatever comes into your world. So what do you want to do? You have a choice to make, a good vibration or a bad vibration? You can choose how you react to people it's your choice.

When someone asks you how are you feeling today you have a choice to feel good or bad. You can either say I do not feel too good today or say I feel like a million pounds.

What you are saying to them is that you consciously have chosen to put yourself in that vibration good or bad you have chosen it.

We have put ourselves in the vibration knowingly. On a knowing level, we refer to vibration as feeling.

We cause, what we feel as we are the ones that allow it. Most people blame other people when that is not true, We have allowed other people to affect us, that is reacting not responding. We are in control of our emotions no-one else.

If we chose good thoughts we stay emotionally involved with the good vibrations. That sets up an attractive force that will bring money, it'll bring love, and it will bring abundance, it'll bring health, it'll bring everything.

Everything is here, nothing is created or destroyed, it is already here. Understanding the law of vibration and everything comes right and sticks. Understanding the law of vibration is a key element in getting what it is you want.

I know I have spoken a lot about manifesting what you want, I see it as part of changing our autopilot, we have to know what is it we want before making changes and be accepting of those changes.

A tree loses its leaves every year in the autumn but it grows new leaves in the spring, life for the tree moves on when it has lost its leaves and regrows more leaves which has a different pattern on or the veins are in a slightly different position to the leaves it has lost.

Everything goes through changes even us humans from when we are born all the way to our deathbed where our souls move on to the afterlife.

Before setting up your vibration or changing your vibration you must know what you want and what your goal is before going after it. What is your end goal?

Whatever it is be on the vibration of love, gratitude, peace and joy, and be happy. Be happy and at peace with who you are and be in the know that it is happening and whatever you want is coming to you and you are making your way to the goal.

Say if I wanted £50 which is a nice low amount to start off with I would simply put a £50 note in my mind's eye, I will go and relax on my bed, close my eyes and imagine £50 coming towards me and landing in my purse. That way I am putting myself in that vibration and one way or another that money would come to me, but I would have to put some work in, in order to get it.

I did this to help me conceive my daughter I would see myself with her, I did this every single time I really wanted something. I will be doing the same thing to get myself published again and anything that I want, this is the way I do it, it sets up the vibration I need to be on and bam I'm on that vibration and I set to work.

If I get stuck I just simply ask the divine for guidance, I receive the guidance in one form or another they may just talk directly to me or show me signs or a like bell goes off in my head when I'm watching something on TV which is when I'm most relaxed.

There is no set time frame for things to come into reality. If you really want a good book to read other than this one about changing paradigms then 'Change your paradigm, change your life' by Bob Proctor is a good book to read.

I have not long given you an excellent way to manifesting or changing your vibration through relaxation/meditation. You can even have motivational posters to change your vibration which is another great way.

You may have a different way of changing your vibration to me. Either way is right there is no wrong way to changing your vibration. When you do it is a great feeling. I had to do it today just to pull myself together and it is ok to feel like rubbish and not do anything. At the end of the day as long as you do something so the day or week is not wasted!!

You can snap out of it, when you are aware of it. The more you do it the easier it becomes and soon it will come as second nature to change how you feel and do stuff.

Understanding the law of vibration will be just a habit and second nature to you so everything falls into place at the right time. You just got to know what it is you want. That is up to you, no one else can decide for you.

It's up to you on what vibration you go on you decide that, bad/poorly vibration or good/healthy vibration, I know which one I will choose. I know this is a lot to take in that is why you reread a book because you cannot take it in all in one go. Your mind and brain has to process this information.

It has to make sense of it all and put it in the right order otherwise it will not work and you will say it doesn't work. The reason it doesn't work is because it is not in the right order. I have purposely not put it in the right order so you can have a play and work things out. I have given you the ingredients, you just have to sort the rest.

It is more fun when you experiment you will learn more quicker and easier, learn from your mistakes, invent games for yourself to learn this stuff and add fun into the mix.

Which will in turn raise your vibration. Another great way to raise your vibration is to put on your favourite music and have a dance, in words of strictly come dancing at the end of their show 'Keep dancing' it raises your vibration.

Do a happy dance or make one up, you never know it could turn into the next dance craze. Get out there and have yourself some fun. Life is not meant to be serious 24/7. Go on let your hair down even if you don't have any!!

What a great way to raise your vibrations, just by having fun. Go into the dream world and fantasise how you want your life to be, feel those emotions and bring them forth into this reality.

I have done all of the above in my life and the good stuff did come my way after I raised my vibration. By raising your vibration you are sending a signal out to the universe saying that you want more of that, please and guess what more will come.

On that note, it does not matter what vibration you are on. You are saying to the universe more of this please, and guess what the universe says 'Your wish is my command' and sends you more of the vibration you are in.

So best to keep your vibrations as high as you can without any aids lol. Yes, it's good to have a balance, but remember to have lots of fun in life. The good stuff will surely flow to you.

When my husband passed over to the afterlife, I was in a bad place and I found it hard to get to the good place where I am now, back to where I was when I first my husband but with a lot more knowledge and thus a different person I have come out of that black tunnel and seen the light and this is what I want for others that are in that black tunnel but unable to see the light vibration this is what I am passing on.

I have been through some dark rubbish and do not want to be there again I have come too far just to turn back around now, but now I am that shining light for someone else.

What did pull me through that horrible tunnel, it was hope. Someone gave me hope to carry on, spirits and angels gave me that hope to carry on and told me I have work to do. I was ready to go over to the other side and be with my husband.

They said no, your work on earth is not done yet you must stay on earth for a bit longer. When raising your vibration in relaxation mode think about a little dial and on that dial are colours and numbers. The numbers are ranging from 1000 to 0.

The dial has four sections 1000 - 750 is the colour of green grass, 749-500 is the colour of dry grass, 499 - 250 is the colour of a sunflower and 249 - 0 is the colour of human blood.

Then you have two little needles, one is pointing to the vibration you want and the other is pointing to the vibration that you are at. Now imagine the needle pointing at where you are at, imagine it moving to the place on the dial that you want it to be.

You should now be feeling your emotions and vibrations change to the desired vibration. Keep focused on that vibration for as long as you can. The longer you do this for the easier it becomes to stay in that vibration in the waking world. Of course, that is up to you on which vibration you choose.

17

Chapter 17 : Decision

Decision is another important aspect of manifesting or the law of attraction. You must make a decision quickly doesn't matter about money or time. Make a decision and stick to it.

Money and time will come if you have the faith that it will happen. With decision comes determination that you want will come to pass as you get to do the doing (taking action).

It doesn't take long to make a decision about 30 secs or less. The quicker you make a decision the less doubt you have about it.

Don't procrastinate, I did that for years, and I still do it occasionally. It's so easy to procrastinate, I'm a master at it lol.

If only we could get paid for procrastinating laugh out loud. Unfortunately, we don't. So time to choose what you want, take action and get paid for what you want to do.

We make decisions all the time, We make a decision when we want a cup of tea or go out for a meal, eat in or out everyday is full of decision making. We make the decision to answer the phone or not, what I am going to eat tonight.

There is not one day that goes by that we do not make a decision. There is also advanced decision making and that is more to do with religion. But still, some people so do that anyway without religion, I am not poking at religion here let that be said. I am just saying some advanced decisions may or may not depend on your religion. It's up to you what you believe I am not forcing you to do anything.

Some people make advanced decisions like going out to meet a friend for example. You go meet them for a drink and they turn around and say you may have something to eat but I am not because I am on 24 hour fast so no food for me, that is the advanced decision she made, she did not make that decision on the spot she had made it in advance of our meeting. So when the time came she did not have to make that decision.

Many people have their reasons for advanced decision-making. It could be a holiday or moving home. You make an advance decision for having a baby or getting married. There is a lot of advanced decisions, and a lot of decision-making on the spot as well. Like making a brew and such like, you may go to the pub and decide there what you are having to drink or may have already thought about what you are going to drink.

Decision-making is something we do everyday without thinking. Like me, I made a committed decision to write this book and get finished by a certain date. I have stuck to that decision and got on with working on it, I even made a plan of how many words I shall write a day to reach this goal.

I made several conscious decisions to make this piece of work. Save money where I can. We make subconscious decisions as well when we are on autopilot. Things we do out of habit and when walking around like zombies!! and need sleep.

Some of us are always on autopilot and have problems just getting into gear. This stuff can be confusing at the start and a lot to take in. A lot of tea is being drunk in the process of creating this book lol.

That includes food as it is a lot for me to write as I am new to this writing game and I did make that committed decision to get this book done by a certain date and I will do it. I am determined to do it. I have been on it long enough, I was struggling at the start to even get words on the page, I had help from Bob Proctor and his colleagues, I had to channel them.

Learn more about the subject and each section as I went. I will keep learning about this and teach it. I love it. As I go through and continue writing about it, it is becoming easier.

Just last week it took me ages to write 3,000 words and it was scary for me to write that many in one day as it seemed like a lot of words to me, but now it is just a drop in the ocean now. It is not scary for me anymore.

Now I'm ok with it, it isn't so scary now I have done it a few times and it's becoming a habit for me, I made a conscious decision to change a habit, instead of lazing around I decided to work on my book and get it done I have been procrastinating enough on it.

Only because I thought it was hard but I changed my thinking on it, and told myself it is easy, and it will get easier, I told myself that chapter is going to be easy because I love that subject and I know about it.

I could of made the decision to sit in front of the TV and not do any writing then I would of had to do a lot more writing tomorrow which obviously would have been double the workload when I have other things to get done and would not get the time to do so.

The only thing is when I start writing I cannot stop writing. It just pours out of me. I have to tell myself off sometimes to stop procrastinating as that will not earn me any money. People are waiting for that book and the universe wants it out there on the book selves. So people can get this help.

Another reason for me procrastinating is that it is scary for me to publish my works it brings tears of pride when I do publish, I am so proud of myself for pushing myself as I was the one that made that decision to publish and become a published author, that for me is shockingly scary.

Now I am getting closer to the end I can feel my heart start to race and breathing is starting to go shallow and a big lump of pride is in my throat, my heart is skipping a beat, and my hands are shaking from the nerves.

It's like falling in love all over again, I made the decision to do this through. I am so close now all I want now is to get it finished and it out there so much so that I could be working on this night and day.

I'm thinking housework can be put on hold, for now, but that can wait, just get this book finished I am so close. I made the decision that I will stick to the plan anyway as it is only a couple of days away from being finished and the housework needs to be done and that means I can celebrate a bit more when I have it complete.

And it will feel a lot better then and I feel even more excited that it is finished and I can start on my next book which is for children and I have asked my daughter to do the illustrations for me, as she loves painting and drawing.

My Mom gave up professional dancing to raise me and my big brother that is one big decision she had to make, her decision to either bring me and my brother up or keep dancing professionally was a major decision she had to make.

She sacrificed her career to raise her family, which to me is a big decision and I don't think she made that decision on her own, but she may well of done but the decision was ultimately hers and hers alone.

Making decisions can be hard and can be easy depending on your preferences, what is important to you, your family or your career? What if you love them both, well in today's world we can have them both, we balance work life with home life it can become a juggling act lol.

Which what I am doing I have a dog to look after on my own and look after a flat while working on my career as an author. I make time to write and look after my home and my dog Edith. It is still a juggling act and then you have visitors when do they come round to visit and how long are they staying that decision is again up to you, your choice.

Your decision, your choice, and the way you live is ultimately up to you. No-one can make you go to work but if you want money and freedom then you'll have to earn it one way or the other. At the end of the day the decision is yours for money or not.

We may feel that the decision is being made for us like the rise in the cost of living, all the prices going up. We still make the last decision to pay or not. The way they think is if you want it you will pay for it. How you want to live is your choice.

Everything we say and do is up to us, we have the power to change the way we think and act. The power is within us and no-one can take that away, look inside you at the power inside, feel it tingling along your skin, on your hands. It is wonderful.

We have an energy field around us just think of the times when someone tried sneaking up behind you to make you jump but you felt them before they even touched you, that is two energy fields coming together.

I know I have gone off subject slightly here, but I had to get that off my chest and still tell you some examples of decision-making we do everyday and some of the big decisions we make at the end of the day we all make decisions whether we like it or not.

We make on average 35,000 decisions a day, that is a lot of decisions many of which we may not know about, so in my thinking, a good portion of that is on autopilot. So that means we are not thinking about the decisions we are taking day in and day out.

Which are habits we have choices throughout the day about what to do and when to do it. Decisions we do on autopilot are out of habit, can we change our habits in order to change our autopilot? The answer is yes we can.

We can only change one or two habits at a time and it takes on average 21 days to change a habit. I have tried to change so many habits I do not like it has slowed me down, Some of my bad habits that I want to get rid of are still around.

My bad habits that I want gone and no longer serve me are fading into the background, those decisions my subconscious is making to get rid of them as I bring in new habits and change my mindset.

I made the decision to change my mindset years ago it was hard to start with but now it is easier as most of my habits are habitual through my autopilot like getting up in the morning and making a cup of tea before I do anything else.

That is what I do on autopilot when I am still half asleep, I wander into the kitchen and make myself a cup of tea, then go back to bed for awhile. While I wake up fully and get ready to take on the day, that is my autopilot at work. That habit I do not want to change.

18

Chapter 18 : What do you really want

What do you want? Is it money? A new car? A new home? Do you want to live by the Sea in a city or in the countryside?

Do you want to work in a factory or at home? You could work in an office, the media, warehouse, or shop. the possibilities are endless maybe an astronaut?

It's all up to you, whatever you want is possible. You have to decide on whatever it is you want, this doesn't have to be quick you can take your time with this.

I suggest you meditate and look inside yourself and ask yourself what it is you are passionate about, and take some much needed time out for personnel development.

I have talked about this throughout this book in the different subjects. I suggest you take what you found out about yourself in mediation and write it out how you want your life to be like.

After you have written it out carry it with you everywhere, put it somewhere you are going to see it everyday. Slowly it will sink into your subconscious mind and slowly put your body into that vibration and then move you into action, into getting what it is you want or do what you want.

What it is you want is up to you no-one can make the decision for you, they can only advise or make suggestions, they do not have to live with the decisions you make about your life and what you want to do with it, you do thou.

If someone told me this when I was younger I would of believed them and my life would so different to what it is now. Never mind I know about it now. My life is changing because of the decisions I make and my life is my own and no-one else's.

Life can be so different when you take that first step in knowing what you want and taking control of your own life. The feeling is magical just knowing what it is you want and taking control, I love that feeling.

At the end of the film called 'Dare to Dream' and she says that one line I can have all that I want, I am in control of what I receive' I think that is what she says. As she drives down the road in her favourite car.

I resonate with what she is saying so much it brings a tear to my eye every single time I watch it. I can feel the power within me as I too know I can have whatever I want, whenever I want it. All I need to know first is what it is I want, what I really want, for myself and the world.

The feeling of just knowing what you want is powerful, it is a driving force that is really powerful. So what is it that you really want? When you know and you have your goals, plan backwards away from the goal. Then you know what the next step is in going towards your goal.

Like writing a book for me I need to know the ending before I put pen to paper, I then work on the framework which makes the writing easier. And of course what is the aim of the book and why I am writing it. This book is not like fiction writing where you can let your imagination go wild, it is factual and so I must do research and learn this for myself.

Then I put it all together and produce a non-fiction self-help book. Writing this has helped me too if it has helped me it can help you too. Which is the aim of this book.

Look at me again going off track a bit again, laugh out loud. It is part of knowing what it is you want and what you want to do, you can see where my passion is. The time has come to know what is it that you want and do.

Once you know what you want, change your autopilot, your thinking, your habits and your paradigms, which will change the way you act.

Decide on what it is you want, then make it into a goal like I said write it down and put it somewhere, where you are going to see it everyday like on your fridge door, above your bathroom mirror or on the bathroom door!! Just make it where you will see it daily.

As you can see all that I have written about so far has its role to play in your dreams coming into reality and changing your mindset(Autopilot). Changing our autopilot is easy when we think about our autopilot as loads of habits compiled together.

Before we can change the autopilot we must know what we want and what habits we want, just read '7 habits of highly effective people' that's a good book to read about habits of highly effective people.

There is nothing much I can say on this subject from what I have already said as it says in the subtitle 'What do you really want?' that is enterally up to you, that's your decision no-one else's.

For years I had an inkling of what I wanted to do and what I wanted, yes a good chunk of it is of shiny material items the dream life of living in a mansion with super fast cars on the gravel driveway then you have some supercars in a big fancy garage.

Yes, that still appeals to me, why is that? Probably because I come from a poverty background and money has always been tight for me growing up so that sort of lifestyle I like and it appeals to me. I like the idea of it, but I want it in Cornwall surrounded by sea air and farmland.

Go to the beach whenever I want, walk along the beach with my hubby and my little dog, I am sharing this so you can get an idea of what I am talking about and for you it might be different you may want to live in the city but I want to live in the countryside in Cornwall. With my nearest neighbour over half a mile away.

No street lights around that shine into the home all night long so I don't get a good nights sleep because of the light shining into the bedroom. In my dream home in Cornwall, all I can hear at night is wildlife and the sea and not to see anything at night while I am sleeping, then there is no excuse for not sleeping as light usually disturbs me at night.

Edith can run around the garden and have a load of fun. This is one of my dreams, to live in a countryside house or manor if you like then I can put friends and family up when they come to visit.

Sounds nice doesn't it, whatever sounds nice or good to you it is possible for you to have it. Keep your dreams alive in your mind and they will come to pass, keep positive and strong. I am positive and confident that I will have the life I dream of.

Including having a hubby for more than four days, that is not me having a go at my late husband for leaving me for the angels above because he was very poorly and I did not know then what I know now.

I will be learning this stuff until pass on over as it is fascinating to me and I love learning about it, I will never cease to stop learning, that will keep me young at heart. This is what I want for my soul, it makes my heart, body and soul sing.

It's in my soul to keep learning and teaching, passing this information on in one form or another to help others, I love it. I live for it. I could write all day and all night but still have other things in my life to take care of including my love life, have some time away from writing books and enjoy what life has to offer.

At this present time of writing this book I am happy and at peace with where I am living because I am zoning out while I write, and I am in my zone of writing so whatever is going on around me is not bothering me. I have shut it all out including what the time is.

All I care about at this moment in time is this book and getting it finished because I cannot wait until it hits the shelves and helps other people, as that is what I want right now in this moment. I am bringing that dream into reality it is my number one goal to reach and I am within touching distance of the finish line.

That feels amazing and that is keeping me going, driving me forward to finishing. So I ask you again as I have shared some private stuff with you, what do you really want? And it can be anything positive.

Do not do this lightly, I want you to really think deep down about what is it that you want, and what habits are stopping you from getting to that dream goal. Which habit is to go first? What new habit are you to start doing in order for your dream to become a reality?

Whatever your dream goal is work backwards from it to find the habits you must possess in order for that dream goal to become a reality, what do you need? Write it all down, it helps to get it clear in your mind if you write it down with a pen and paper and do not type it out.

It sinks in quicker and better if you write it and not type it. This sets up the vibration in your subconscious and keeps watering that seed and eventually, your body will be in the same vibration and be turning that seed into results.

When I did not do this, it was a hard graft of blood sweat, swearing and tears to get what I wanted, to change my mindset and autopilot. When I did write my dream goals down it sank in quicker and easier.

Now I am always doing it, it's like the universe reads what you write and grants it quicker. Plus your mind is also reading what you put on the paper, it is as if you are burning it into your mind.

Whatever you want is possible no matter what anyone else tells you, Write a load of positive sayings, all the positive things people will be saying when you have reached your dream goal. All you have to do at this point is imagine all those positive sayings people are going to say to you.

Imagine people coming up to you and congratulating you, shaking your hand and giving you hugs. Wow, what a feeling!! keep that feeling inside you. Sometimes it is good not to share and keep your cards close to your chest, until it is time to share with the world what you have done. Unlike me I find it hard to keep my mouth shut when I am so excited about something. I have to bite my tongue to stop myself.

It is easy to get caught up in the moment, and everything comes spilling out!! I am very excitable when I plan things. When people are negative to me all I want to do in order to shut them up is tell them what is happening and tell them my exciting news and plans, something that is positive to counteract their negativity. I end up stumbling over my own words in my excitement, laugh out loud. It's all good because then they don't understand what you said or what you are talking about.

19

Chapter 19 : Confidence

So who do you want to become? the choice is yours. No-one can push you around unless you let them.

I too have let people push me around for too long. I have changed that one too many times and it never stuck, this time I choose what I want and it's going to stick.

As I have said in the past from a young age I wanted to become an author but didn't know what to write I was a confused little girl. I always knew I wanted to be a writer/Author but I was put in a box and told I cannot do it as I was too thick to do it. I've shown them and the fact is that I was told I would never be able to drive, but now I can drive and have a car.

Never ever let anyone put you in a box and tell you, that you cannot do something when you are more than capable of doing it.

I can go on at this forever and a day but only you can choose who you want to become. I choose to be a positive person alongside a lovely personality who would get on with anyone as long as they respect me lol. I am just learning to respond and not react as I can have a short fuse if I'm overtired.

I love positive me, I love being positive and no-one is going to tell me any different, I am my own person. So one question remains for you. Who do you want to become... What and who are you leaving behind when you pass over to the other side?

Do you want to leave a legacy behind what are people going to say about you when you go over to the other side? Now you know what it is you want and who you to become next is the confidence, if you do not have the confidence to go forward how are you going to achieve your dreams and dream goals?

This is what this chapter is for, to help you gain confidence in yourself, as I too was not very confident in getting my goals, as I have mentioned I was always put down and I was surrounded by negative people. I have now moved on from them and I surrounded myself with positive people and it has taken some doing to stop thinking negatively and start being positive.

This is what I did to gain confidence in myself, I surrounded myself with positive people and I kept the negative people at arm's length, I did daily affirmations including this affirmation ' I am Strong and confident' I even said them in the bathroom mirror. I said them out loud so it would sink in even quicker plus I wrote them down over and over again.

I thought to myself the only thing that matters is what I think, I was one of these people that was trying to please everyone and not thinking for myself, I was saying yes to everyone not giving it any thought to what I wanted, I was too busy trying to please everyone. Until one day I thought to myself I cannot please everyone and only I matter and make myself happy and those around me should follow suit.

My happiness counts, then I found myself thinking about what made me happy which was obvious it is helping others, and how I am to help others and what else do I love. I love writing I know what I will do, I will write a book focusing on helping people.

Every time I am not feeling confident I ask myself why am I not feeling confident, if I am just frightened of the outcome I just remind myself why I doing what I am doing.

I also do a little power move like punching the air and saying to myself I can do this, there is nothing stopping me from doing it. I have the will power and determination to do it. I am worthy of having all that I want in life, there is nothing wrong with me I am perfect. I have this poster on my wall too so I can read it out loud to myself as well.

With this, I am building my confidence with the help of my positive friends and my mentors. The people I look up to and want to be like them. I have lots of positive and motivational posters around my flat including a vision wall instead of a vision board. It drives me forward towards my goals.

I have pictures of the material things I want on my walls like a child who has posters of their favourite band or car, it reminds me of my dreams that includes my mission statement and my plans so I can see them everyday.

I will talk a little bit on the mission statement here now just so you know all companies have mission statements and everybody should be involved in the mission statement and should be available to all employees. If you want to know more about mission statements then I suggest you read 7 habits of highly effective people, highly effective people have mission statements.

There are different ways of gaining confidence that way I have just told you about which worked for me, I also tell myself that everything is going to be ok and they are not going to judge me, and if they do so what does it matter? Am I going to see them and speak to them?

If you are going to see them or speak to them face to face, do a fist pump and say to yourself I can do this, I have this in the bag! There is nothing wrong with me I am perfect. Feel the power come from within, and getting out of your comfort zone helps you grow your confidence.

When I started doing vlogs on YouTube I was nervous as anything I kept muddling up my words and I even prepared what I was going to say and I even rehearsed saying it, it took several out-takes to get it right.

I pushed myself out of my comfort zone, to do that. I then started to become more confident the more I did it, now I am happy with being in front of the camera as I was camera shy before even going on stage in front of 35,000 people with cameras in my face I was camera shy then but I hid it well and as I didn't have to talk.

The more push yourself out of your comfort zone the more your confidence will grow, When I first joined 4N which is a networking group for business people and you get one chance per meeting to stand up and talk about your business in 60 seconds or less. Now as this was public speaking I was frightened to do this, I even had notes of what I was going to say.

It was like standing up in class half naked and talking about something, so I even stumbled over my words then as I was way out of my comfort zone but the more I did it, the easier it became to talk in front of strangers and those I have met before and spoke to on a one to one level instead of the whole class.

I was more comfortable with the one-to-one meeting instead of standing and speaking to a group of 15-35 people. I still get nervous now but I am no longer so frightened that I trip over my own words. I am gaining confidence with my videos as they are getting longer and longer as I go.

The next step for me is to talk to the camera while I am out and about, which I am nervous about and editing the video as I keep thinking what if it is not good enough what are people going to think, what are they going to say, are they going to be mean and nasty.

Yes, I am a published Author but that does not stop the nerves, I have just got to be brave and take the plunge as I did with my first book. I will be going to do what I have said in this book about confidence and push myself out of my comfort zone.

I will be doing my power move, giving myself courage and asking for some reassurance from my friends and from the universe. I'll close my eyes and jump!! That is what it is like for me lol.

If you want confidence then just follow what I said at the start and in next to no time you will of gained confidence. Once you are over the fear and got used to that comfort zone that you just made. It is time to push yourself even more to the next level.

Then you can keep pushing yourself on to the next level, once you get passed one level chances are you going to feel empowered to move on to the next level and will be feeling pumped to move on and push yourself again and again.

Before you know it your confidence will be through the roof. I have done this many times over and I get such a rush after getting through my terror barrier and then becomes the norm for me then I push myself again.

I am falling in love with doing it, it is the way to grow, just like learning a new skill. It is scary at first then it is ok and you get over the fear. Like going somewhere new for an example going to a new job or starting a new school, being the newbie!

There is a first time for everything, like riding a bike. Once you get the hang of it, it's easy like driving a car, once you learned those life skills they are there for life always.

When I fell off my bike and head-butted the pavement my confidence was knocked out of me after trying to be brave but I got back on my bike and carried on cycling once I was better and the wounds were healed apart from the confidence that had been knocked out of me until many years later and realised what happened and I put the pieces of the puzzle together.

Confidence comes from your belief in yourself as well and you can become confident, and believe in yourself that you can do stuff. You are more than capable of doing them, surround yourself with positive people and those who love giving out hugs which can be a confidence booster.

Hugs are like reassurance without any spoken words of encouragement. Like I said get a positive mentor or life coach that is willing to help you. The more hugs the more you can give out as well and more will come back to you with lots more positive energy.

Confidence is amazing when you have it, all you need is a little bit to start with and it will grow and grow as push yourself out of your comfort zone, your life will change and your autopilot will be changing too.

Gaining confidence improves your life and those around you, I think you understand by now, I hope and I have given food for thought here too. Something to work on if you are not very confident.

Don't forget what your very first step is, Know what it is you want to do, and what do you want your life to look like, what are you surrounded by. Who is in your life?

Without knowing what it is you want how can ask for it or go after it? So that is very vital you know this. Then write it down and put it where you will see it every single day. It will then be a daily reminder for you and slowly sink in and become part of you.

20

Chapter 20 : Law of Attraction

The law of attraction is a secondary law, after The law of Vibration. The Law of Vibration is a primary law like the law of gravity.

To get to the law of attraction we must in turn set up the vibration and get in harmony with what we want.

When we get in the vibration of what we want, we are in turn attracting like a magnet to what we want.

Everything that you are seeking seeks you in return. Everything you want is already yours. So you can get anything. It's just a matter of becoming more aware of what you already possess.

When you bring your life into harmony with the divine order. You will actually find the "negative" will have moved on, as its cause would have been removed, and you would no longer attract what don't want.

The results you desire in the physical realm, are locked into the law of attraction, I created this book with the help of Bob Proctor's teachings and his book called "You Were Born Rich". I am putting the teaching in a way that, people with dyslexia, and learning difficulties understand "the secret" and people attract what they want.

I want to help people understand this and give something positive into the world. After getting into harmony with what you want and you are attracting what you want, then the chances are it's going to go away again unless you stay in that vibration and your results will then stick to you like honey.

I have taken a leaf out of Bob Proctor's book for this next bit about an acorn that he used in seminars and in his book 'You Were Born Rich' Page 124.

Keep in mind that everything in the universe you can see with the naked eye and everything cannot see, this is an expression of spirit. Please bear in mind that Spirit operates by exact laws. We are subject to those laws as we are spirits experiencing a human existence.

Bob Proctor in his book 'You Were Born Rich' says "For years I have held up an acorn in the seminar and used it as a device for helping people to gain a better understanding of how the law of attraction works in their lives. So Please visualise, if you will, an acorn. Then think-really think about what it is you are looking at."

The acorn may appear solid, but you must understand the acorn is not solid and is a mass of molecules at a very high rate of vibration. In the acorn, there is a nucleus or a patterned plan which tells the vibratory rate, of how fast it moves.

The same principle holds true for all seeds. All seeds have a nucleus or patterned plan in order to grow. It tells vibratory how fast to vibrate.

You maybe aware of this fact: Everything is governed by law and I do not mean the actual government who says what you have to pay and where to and where taxes go. I mean the law of the universe, Karma if you will. There is a basic law where nothing gets created or destroyed just changes form.

Take this for an example: If something is not in the process of growing, it must be, by the law of its being, must be dying. Like the acorn out of the soil, it must be decaying very slowly. Put the acorn in soil and water it and the vibratory rate changes by the nucleus or patterned plan now it is set up in order to grow and expand. As it's vibrating at this rate which it attracts what is vibrating in harmony with it. If you were able to see it with the naked eye, what is taking place, you would see "a parade" of particles of energy-never ending stream of them in an orderly fashion to the acorn. They connect to the molecules to grow and expand, then become larger and grow.

I say you must act, think, believe, and feel as if you are already in possession of what you want. I could go on and on with Bob's words and try and make it sound better to those who have learning difficulties and dyslexia like I have but I won't as it will only get too complicated and you will not understand I can only just understand it with my limited knowledge of science as my high school science is none existent. I was ungraded on all of my science exams I only just scraped through mainstream school with minimal assistance.

I want to share this knowledge that I have learned from Bob and gang of successful and wealthy people and pass it on to those less fortunate who either don't understand, or haven't heard it or think it's a load of crap because it hasn't worked for them for one reason or another.

When you have this knowledge and know-how to apply it, it works and the next task is making it stick, which comes with habits and changing of your paradigms, and autopilot.

I will say this in order to change your bad habits into good habits that will help you become wealthy. Change 1 or 2 habits at a time, it takes 21 days to change a habit and you must do it everyday without fail so it's down to you if you succeed or fail?!

You have the choice, no-one else only you, Your future is in your hands. And don't forget to study and do it repeatedly to form a new habit. I understand this maybe complicated to some people and then may not be to others. For some it might just finally click.

I am leaving the order as it is for now, I have given you quite a lot of information to digest and also given you a couple of steps in the right order and I will leave the rest up to you so you can experiment with which is part of the learning process.

Remember what I have covered from the start; our conditioning, believing, seeing is not believing, Happiness, the mind, overcoming fears, love, meditation, gratitude, faith, the will, memory, reason, perception, imagination, the law of vibration, decision, what do you really want, confidence and the law of attraction.

That is a lot of information to take in, I suggest you reread this book several times in order to digest it, I would read one chapter at a time and digest that, get your head around it before moving on to the next chapter.

I have experimented with the order and I have finally got it right. Now I am at the stage of keep practising the right order. How else would this book have reached you?

There is nothing more I can really say on the law of attraction, other than what Bob has said and I have changed the wording slightly to try and make it understandable in the English language here in the UK, as the USA and UK English differ a bit and I come from the outskirts of Birmingham so I speak with a Brummie accent.

In plain and simple terms the law of attraction is a magnet, whatever we keep thinking about and we put ourselves on that vibration we will attract whatever is on that vibration. As I have said the law of attraction is secondary law and the law of vibration is a primary law. We can not change this.

The law of attraction is like a magnet attracting metal pieces to it. Keep that in mind. Time for you to figure out the order from knowing what it is you want. I am coming to the end of the book now.

After setting up the vibration in your mind and your autopilot of what it is you want, your body, brain and mind will go to work and bring it into reality for you. You maybe seeing what we mean when we say the law of vibration is the primary law and the law of attraction is a secondary law.

After knowing what it is you want, next is writing this out and putting it somewhere, where you are going to see it daily. Next is meditating and asking for guidance. While in the meditative state put yourself onto the vibration of what it is you want.

I'm sure you can figure the rest out for yourself, it is easy. I have done this many times now, some I have done when I was unaware of this law of attraction business. Some I have done when I became aware of it.

Things you can do when you are aware of it. And putting it all in the right order. I'll leave this chapter here and move on to the summary now.

Summary

There is a lot of information in this book and with the help of Bob's teachings. I have put this book together in order to help others who are struggling in changing their autopilot so they can manifest what they want in their lives.

Some may not have heard about this or thought it is a load of rubbish and a lot of nonsense and make-believe. I know differently because I have made it work for me, I may not be rich or famous but I have now two books out and that is what I wanted.

I set the vibration up in my mind and worked on my autopilot and I published this book to help others and that is what I have gone and done with my mind and body in harmony with each other.

I have been determined to get it out and get it finished by a certain date and I have managed it. It may have been tough going at some points, but I got through it.

Time to get out of your comfort zone, decide on what it is you want and go for it. If I can do it so can you. So reread this book as you might have missed some bits as we all do. That is another reason to repeat.

Have you ever watched a movie once and watched it again and there are bits you didn't see the first time you watched it? Then you watch the movie again and you see things you didn't see the second time you watched it?

I hear you ask why is this? it's because of the chatter going on in our brains, and focusing on something for that amount of time is nearly impossible for our brains to do. So our brains do zone out and come back in again so quickly that we do not notice that it is doing it, and it does it on autopilot. Which is possible to change.

Go ahead and make your dreams come true. You can do it, I have faith in you. Don't let anyone tell you, you cannot do it because you can, Listen to your heart and soul. You have this.

Now it is time for a change, are you going up or down? It's your choice which way you go. I choose up, as I have been down, down to rock bottom and it is not a nice place to go. If I were you I would choose to go up. You have the power within you, just look in your heart.

Love always to you, my friend xx

My Other Books

I have only written one other book I do have more planned in the future.

Ups and Downs of Life.

www.ingramcontent.com/pod-product-compliance
Lightning Source LLC
Chambersburg PA
CBHW060634290526
45793CB00001B/246